From Process To Product: Beginning—Intermediate Writing Skills For Students of ESL

From Process to Product: Beginning—Intermediate Writing Skills for Students of ESL

NATALIE LEFKOWITZ
University of Washington

Illustrated by
Lori Weisenfeld

Prentice Hall Regents, Englewood Cliffs, NJ 07632

Library of Congress Cataloging-in-Publication Data

Lefkowitz, Natalie, 1954–
From process to product.

1. English language—Text-books for foreign speakers. I. Title.
PE1128.L453 1986 809.3 86-3201
ISBN 0-13-331-695-5

Editorial/production supervision and interior design: Janis Oppelt
Manufacturing buyer: Harry P. Baisley

Printed in the United States of America
10 9 8 7 6 5

ISBN 0-13-331695-5

Prentice-Hall International (UK) Limited, *London*
Prentice-Hall of Australia Pty. Limited, *Sydney*
Prentice-Hall Canada Inc., *Toronto*
Prentice-Hall Hispanoamericana, S.A., *Mexico*
Prentice-Hall of India Private Limited, *New Delhi*
Prentice-Hall of Japan, Inc., *Tokyo*
Prentice-Hall of Southeast Asia Pte. Ltd., *Singapore*
Editora Prentice-Hall do Brasil, Ltda., *Rio de Janeiro*

To my mother, Selma Lefkowitz,
and my father,
Murray Lefkowitz

Contents

Preface

From Process to Product is a writing text for students of English as a second language. It presents communicative practice in the skills needed for both the writing process and its developing product. Though primarily directed toward beginning students, the text can be adapted to intermediate and even advanced students since the writing process is essentially the same at all levels. The book encourages writing based on students' experiences and actively promotes a combination of communicative content, organization, and grammar, which is supported by examples based on the author's life. At times, the contents are geared toward university-bound students, but enough material is provided to satisfy any adult ESL writer.

Acknowledgements

It would be difficult to enumerate all of the influences that figure in the making of a person, a teacher, a writer and a book. From the beginning of the long process of writing *From Process to Product* through the final revisions of the completed manuscript, I have been affected by many friends and colleagues. I'd like to take this opportunity to express my gratitude to the following people, who directly or indirectly contributed to the realization of this dream.

- My many international students, whose appreciation and support have been my greatest reward.
- Paul Schneider, Chaouky Kaboul and Alberto Campero for their encouragement during the early stages of the project and for their confidence in my professional abilities.
- Debbie Dohrmann, Pat Dwyer, Ed Gilday, John Hedgcock, Patty Heiser, Virginia Holman, Candace Jarrett, Barbara Peterson, John Roberts, and Herb Sundvall, talented colleagues, with whom I have shared support, enthusiasm, insights and laughter.
- Kathie Connolly and Lindsay Michimoto for their professional typing of the manuscript.
- Betty Azar, whose work I so admire, and Caroline Campbell, for their detailed and insightful examination of the first version of the manuscript.
- Caroline Mark and Stewart Gardner for their friendship and sound advice.
- Sandra Silberstein, valued friend, professor, ESL instructor, administrator and author, who found time in her busy schedule to provide me with constant feedback and encouragement. She shared my struggle when I needed someone and contributed to every aspect of the revision process.
- Lori Weisenfeld, sensitive and skillful illustrator, who so cleverly captured with pictures, what I had intended with words.
- Robin Baliszewski and Brenda White, ESL Acquisition Editors, Susan Rowan, Assistant Acquisition Editor, and Janis Oppelt, Production Editor, as well as the readers and production staff at Prentice-Hall.
- My mother and father, and Lucas, for being everything you are to me.

Notes to the Teacher

From Process to Product combines practice in the skills needed for both the writing process and its resulting product. The purpose of the book is to make writing a pleasant experience, rather than an overwhelming task for beginning students of ESL. At the same time, it presents a simple approach to you which makes the teaching of writing equally enjoyable.

Students often fear writing, even in their own language, because of the number of things they must pay attention to simultaneously. When asked to concentrate on grammar, students often ignore content. When given the freedom to explore their creativity, their grammar suffers. This book demonstrates that the process of writing combines content, organization, grammar, and revision, with an eye toward a final product. Structure and creativity are neither incompatible nor mutually exclusive. Unfortunately, they have traditionally been presented as such. Writing instruction should incorporate all aspects of the composing process, as well as examples of the desired product. Creative communicative competence need not preclude grammaticality and organization. In fact, clear examples will provide the necessary input for all of these facets.

This book encourages students to experience the process of writing by combining creative content with focused grammar and rhetorical devices. The initial chapter of the book, The Planning Process, is devoted to brainstorming skills that develop gradually—beginning with unstructured tasks and moving on to more structured kinds of tasks. Brainstorming as an independent practice evolves into brainstorming combined with outlining. Finally, the focus shifts to the use of outlines. The outlining section introduces students to some basic organizational skills such as distinguishing generals from specifics; using different kinds of ordering; developing topics, concluding sentences, and the body of the paragraph; and sticking to the assigned topic. A full elaboration of rhetorical devices is presented in Chapter 2, which is devoted to the processes of Refining and Revising. Exercises are carefully assigned to provide contextualized practice. This chapter includes connectors such as those that show addition, result, opposition, examples, similarity, summary, time, chronological sequence, spatial relationships, and emphasis. The next part teaches organizational strategies and rhetorical devices. The last part focuses on various approaches to correction.

Chapter 3, The Product through Process: Composing Paragraphs, is, in many ways, the core of the book. It centers on the culmination of the writing process—the product itself. At this point, students will have developed personalized writing approaches that they can apply to actual paragraphs. This section helps students to incorporate and synthesize the skills of the composing process. Creative compositions with outlines illustrate different rhetorical devices and grammar, as a point of departure for stimulus, guidance, and support. These paragraphs are realistic in that they serve as models which exemplify low-level grammar in authentic, rather than artificially contrived, situations. In addition, the choice of topics is experientially based, allowing students to focus on content rather than grammar. The grammar will emerge naturally, since it is being applied to realistic settings. In much the same way that grammar can be conceptualized, so can patterns of organization. Students will be better prepared to internalize rhetorical devices after having learned them in the planning process and seen them presented in model compositions. The models are not designed for the purpose of copying but, rather, as resources of comprehensible input which promote self-confidence and encourage natural language. They provide clear examples of the author's experience. It is then up to the students to share their own similar, though not identical, experiences. The writer's focus is thus on the process as well as the product, since the two are intricately intertwined.

Experience is the key to creativity. Students will not be overwhelmed when asked to draw from their own experiences. Creativity will naturally surface when students retell something they have lived. In addition, the topics for each composition have been chosen because they lend themselves comfortably to the assigned grammar. Therefore, the pressure of thinking about topics while focusing on structure is removed from the students. The responsibility of creating appropriate writing topics is also removed from you, the instructor.

Because this book is geared toward the beginning student of ESL, most of the outlined compositions are limited to one paragraph of about eight sentences. This limitation helps students to avoid the problem of writing either excessive or insufficient amounts. However, limitations are merely suggested. Although students might benefit from adhering to strict limitations at first, with your assistance they will recognize when they are ready to expand their writing and deviate from the guidelines presented. For students who feel confident and ready to advance, examples of expanded paragraph compositions are presented in Chapter 4. Hopefully, when students become comfortable with the process of creating one paragraph, they will be able to understand that three, five, or any number of paragraphs that constitute a final product, result from the same writing process.

The material in this book is easy for you to present. The Contents show the evolution of the planning process to its ultimate stage—the product—and are designed to be taught in that order. However, you might find another order which is better suited to your classroom needs. For example, there are sections in Chapters 1, 2, and 3 which overlap. You might choose to teach them together, or separate them as I have, for the purpose of cyclical review. All exercises are self-explanatory. Your task, therefore, is to guide students through the process exercises before worrying about the final product. When it is time to concentrate on the product, you should be sure that they are familiar with the important grammar focus points. For your assistance, a brief contextualized review of the target grammar precedes each model paragraph. It would be helpful to your students if you reviewed these paragraphs together in class, discussing content, vocabulary, and organization in addition to grammar. Drawing your students' attention to the illustrations provided will enhance their understanding of these paragraphs. You will also find a review of typical problem areas for non-native English speakers in the appendices.

The inspiration for *From Process to Product* is both a love of writing and teaching and a great respect for individual creativity. Writing is a wonderful means of self-expression which, with a little practice, is available to most people. Focusing on personal experience in a manageable format allows for imaginative, enjoyable compositions, which are well-organized and grammatically precise. Topics based on the students' own perceptions will elicit high levels of motivation, creativity, and interest. In this process of combining different aspects of writing, neither ideas nor forms are excessively emphasized, but instead work together as a harmonious unit. Students exercise their own initiative by inventing, organizing, and revising. If this book enables students to appreciate the writing process while learning how to write well, it will achieve its goal. I hope you and your students enjoy this text.

Natalie Lefkowitz

1 The Planning Process

BRAINSTORMING

The first stage in the planning process is called *brainstorming*. Brainstorming involves thinking of as many ideas as you can without worrying about such things as organization or grammar. The purpose of brainstorming is to help free your thoughts, break down mental blocks (the feeling you get when you don't know what to write about), and open your mind to other possible ways of looking at things.

In this section, your teacher will assign you exercises that will give you practice in brainstorming composition topics that you would like to write about, brainstorming ideas about topics that are given to you, and brainstorming topics about ideas that are given to you. To do these exercises, relax and let your mind wander. With your teacher at the blackboard, you might work by yourself or with your classmates.

When you finish these exercises, the next chapter will give you additional practice with brainstorming, but this time the brainstorming will be more focused.

Focus: *Brainstorming Free Composition Ideas*

Think about some topics that interest you and that you would like to write about. *Brainstorm,* or let ideas come to your mind, and write them down as you think of them. You can use one word, or a few words. The important thing is to write as many ideas in this space as you can.

Exercise:

Focus:
Understanding Brainstorming—Ideas for Assigned Topics

First, look at the subject. Then, write a list of everything that comes to your mind about that subject. Follow the example. Then you try it. Your teacher will help you with difficult vocabulary.

Example:

Things that are American stereotypes:

hamburgers	Coca-Cola
football	baseball
apple pie	hot dogs

Now, follow the above example and brainstorm everything that comes to your mind about the following subjects.

Exercise:

Things that are typical of my country:

Things I want to see in the United States:

Things that you wear in my country:

Things that a tourist should visit in my country:

Things that are difficult for a foreigner in a new country:

Things that I left at home that I want to have here:

Focus: *Brainstorming for a Topic—Topics for Assigned Ideas*

Look at the following lists. Choose a *general topic* or *umbrella* for each list and write it in the space provided.

Exercise:

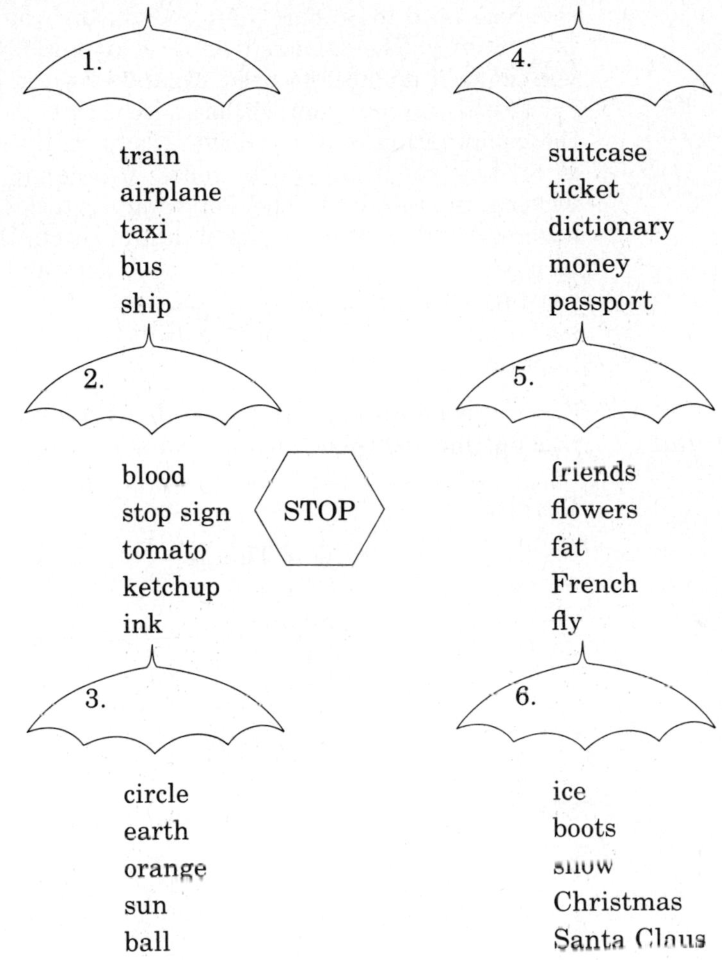

BRAINSTORMING AND OUTLINING

In the previous section, you practiced brainstorming exercises and loosened up your mind. This is similar to stretching before you run. When you exercise, you need to prepare your body before you do a more regulated or organized activity. The same is true for your mind. You need to *get in shape* before you make it do more focused, organized work.

In this section, you will practice the second stage of the planning process, the combination of brainstorming and outlining. The reason you brainstorm is to help you think about ideas in order to become a better writer. Good writing is organized. The following exercises show you ways to use brainstorming for different kinds of organization. If you plan your writing, it will be clear and easy for the reader to understand. One system for planning your writing is called *outlining*. You can practice combining the freedom of brainstorming with the control of outlining in the next pages. This practice leads to paragraph writing.

Focus: *Brainstorming Outlines*

Choose three things that go together from your brainstorm lists and fit them into outline form. Look at the example.

Example:

Hot Things
Sun
Summer
Oven
Coffee
Desert
Spicy food

I. Hot things
  A. Summer
  B. Sun
  C. Desert

Exercise:

I. ____________________
  A. ____________________
  B. ____________________
  C. ____________________

I. ____________________
  A. ____________________
  B. ____________________
  C. ____________________

I. ____________________
  A. ____________________
  B. ____________________
  C. ____________________

I. ____________________
  A. ____________________
  B. ____________________
  C. ____________________

I. ____________________
  A. ____________________
  B. ____________________
  C. ____________________

I. ____________________
  A. ____________________
  B. ____________________
  C. ____________________

Focus: *Developing the Outlines*

Choose the letters A, B, and C from your outline on page 4 and brainstorm as many different ideas about them as possible. Look at the example below.

Example:

I. Hot things		A. Summer	B. Sun	C. Desert
A. Summer		1. Swimming	1. Bright	1. Dry
B. Sun	→	2. Resting	2. Yellow	2. Sandy
C. Desert		3. Vacation	3. Warmth	3. Big
		4. Sleeping	4. Rays	4. Dusty
		5. Suntan	5. Glasses	5. Camel
		6. Beach	6. Pretty	6. Arabia

Exercise:

I. ________		A. ________	B. ________	C. ________
A. ________		1. ________	1. ________	1. ________
B. ________	→	2. ________	2. ________	2. ________
C. ________		3. ________	3. ________	3. ________
		4. ________	4. ________	4. ________
		5. ________	5. ________	5. ________
		6. ________	6. ________	6. ________

I. ________		A. ________	B. ________	C. ________
A. ________		1. ________	1. ________	1. ________
B. ________	→	2. ________	2. ________	2. ________
C. ________		3. ________	3. ________	3. ________
		4. ________	4. ________	4. ________
		5. ________	5. ________	5. ________
		6. ________	6. ________	6. ________

I. ________		A. ________	B. ________	C. ________
A. ________		1. ________	1. ________	1. ________
B. ________	→	2. ________	2. ________	2. ________
C. ________		3. ________	3. ________	3. ________
		4. ________	4. ________	4. ________
		5. ________	5. ________	5. ________
		6. ________	6. ________	6. ________

Focus:
Following the Outline—Sentence Expansion

Choose at least two of your ideas about A, two ideas about B, and two ideas about C. Write complete sentences for each idea. Look at the examples below.

Examples:

A. Summer
1. Beach √
2. Resting
3. Vacation
4. Sleeping
5. Suntan
6. Swimming √

A. Summer
Beach—The sand and ocean are beautiful at the beach.
Swimming—I swim there every afternoon.

B. Sun
1. Yellow
2. Bright √
3. Warmth √
4. Rays
5. Sunglasses
6. Pretty

B. Sun
Bright—The sun makes everything bright and hot.
Warmth—The world is clear and warm on sunny days.

C. Desert
1. Dry √
2. Sandy
3. Big
4. Dusty
5. Camels √
6. Arabia

C. Desert
Dry—The desert is dry so people are thirsty there.
Camels—However, camels don't get thirsty.

On the following lines, take your brainstorm lists from page 5 and choose at least two ideas from letters A, B, and C. Write complete sentences for the ideas you choose.

Exercise:

A. ____________________
1. ____________________
2. ____________________
3. ____________________
4. ____________________
5. ____________________
6. ____________________

A. ____________________________________
__________ — __________________________
__________ — __________________________

B. ____________________
1. ____________________
2. ____________________
3. ____________________
4. ____________________
5. ____________________
6. ____________________

B. ____________________________________
__________ — __________________________
__________ — __________________________

C. ______________________ C. ____

1. ______________________ — ____

2. ______________________ — ____

3. ______________________

4. ______________________

5. ______________________

6. ______________________

OUTLINING AND ORGANIZATION

You have already practiced free brainstorming, as well as controlled brainstorming and have been introduced to outlines and paragraphs. The third stage of the planning process focuses on *outlining*. An outline is simply a plan to follow. It develops from lots of thought and brainstorming. It is difficult to write when you have not planned what you want to say. Without planning, it is easy to write either too much or not enough and hard to present sentences in an organized fashion. If you think of the outline as a road map and the composition as a trip, you will realize that you can get lost if you do not follow the map. Your teacher will show you that the outline is merely a suggested plan and, therefore, does not require many details. The composition will provide details. Similarly, a road map does not always include information about hitchhikers, scenery, gas stations, and different restaurants. These appear in the discussion of the trip. The road map, however, directs the traveler to his or her destination in much the same way that the outline helps writers to reach their goal.

The following is a simple outline for a one-paragraph composition.

Title: ____________________

Introduction: I. ____________________

A. ____________________

Body: B. ____________________

C. ____________________

Conclusion: ____________________

In writing, the unit that is used to express ideas is the *paragraph*. A paragraph has an introductory or topic sentence, a body, and a concluding sentence.

1. **The introductory or topic sentence** introduces (shows, describes, presents, illustrates, gives) an idea. This sentence is *always indented.*
2. **The body** has sentences that support, develop, and describe the idea stated in the topic sentence. There are usually about six sentences that make up the body in a paragraph.
3. **The concluding sentence** concludes (ends, finishes up) the written discussion of the idea or subject that was introduced in the topic sentence.

In the introduction, one *umbrella* or *topic* sentence is written which is general enough to cover the three specific points which are to follow. You should write words in *parallel form* for Specifics A, B, C. In the conclusion, you can summarize, re-emphasize, or reach some kind of solution by writing one complete sentence. The conclusion should remind your reader in a general way about what you have said. See the example on page 9.

In the actual one-paragraph composition, eight complete sentences are suggested. The introduction or first sentence is the same as the one presented in the outline. Then, for each specific point two sentences are suggested. Two sentences for A, two sentences for B, and two sentences for C make up the body of the composition. Finally, the same complete sentence is written in the conclusion as in the outline. The easiest way for you to see the relationship between outline and composition is by looking at a model. A one-paragraph outline and model is provided on page 9. Of course, these are suggested guidelines that can be expanded or limited depending on how much you are ready to write. Your teacher will help you to decide this.

OVERVIEW

Focus: ***Suggested Format***

This model shows the outline and paragraph format you will use as well as the distribution of the suggested eight sentences. Your teacher will go over the outline and model with you and point out focused grammatical structures (modals), new vocabulary, and types of organization (cause and effect). On a separate sheet of paper, you should then write your own outline and composition based on this example. Your purpose here is to practice outline and paragraph form. This time, write eight sentences in your paragraph. Later, you can write more or less as you become experienced.

Example:

Title:	Studying in Another Country
Introduction:	I. There are many good reasons for people to study in a foreign country. (1)
	A. Language (2,3)
Body:	B. Culture (4,5)
	C. People (6,7)
Conclusion:	People can broaden their experience and increase their knowledge by studying outside of their own countries. (8)

Studying in Another Country

1)There are many good reasons for people to study in a foreign country. 2)First, it is a good opportunity for foreign students to learn a new language. 3)In addition, they can practice it every day. 4)Second, they are able to live in a different culture. 5)Therefore, students will learn new customs and traditions. 6)Finally, they will be in contact with new people. 7)They can develop relationships with international friends. 8)People can broaden their experience and increase their knowledge by studying outside of their own countries.

Focus: ***Outline Practice***

Since an outline is like a road map, practice making outlines based on different points on a road map. First look at the examples and then do the same thing from your country or city.

Examples:

I. Houston	II. Texas	III. The Southwestern United States
A. North	A. Dallas	A. Texas
B. South	B. Houston	B. Arizona
C. East	C. San Antonio	C. New Mexico

Now you try the same kind of organization using your cities, directions, states, countries, and continents.

Exercise:

I. ________	II. ________	III. ________
A. ________	A. ________	A. ________
B. ________	B. ________	B. ________
C. ________	C. ________	C. ________
IV. ________	V. ________	VI. ________
A. ________	A. ________	A. ________
B. ________	B. ________	B. ________
C. ________	C. ________	C. ________

Focus: *General and Specific Statements*

Lists of words are provided which you should arrange so that the most general idea is on top. This exercise will help you see that the introductory *umbrella* or *topic* statement must be broad enough to include the specific details of the body. Remember that everything is equal here, so the order of specifics is not important. First position is the same as second and third.

Exercise:

Mother	I.	________
Family		A. ________
Father		B. ________
Child		C. ________

Toyota	I.	________
Pontiac		A. ________
Cars		B. ________
Volkswagen		C. ________

Chair	I.	________
Bed		A. ________
Table		B. ________
Furniture		C. ________

Doctor	I.	________
Occupations		A. ________
Teacher		B. ________
Dentist		C. ________

Elementary	I.	________
Intermediate		A. ________
Levels		B. ________
Advanced		C. ________

Apple	I.	________
Orange		A. ________
Fruits		B. ________
Banana		C. ________

Pretty	I. ____________
Ugly	A. ____________
Cold	B. ____________
Adjectives	C. ____________

Is difficult to park	I. ____________
Disadvantages of a car over a bicycle	A. ____________
Uses gas	B. ____________
Needs more expensive care	C. ____________

Packing a suitcase	I. ____________
Getting traveler's checks	A. ____________
Buying a plane ticket	B. ____________
Preparing for a trip	C. ____________

Focus: *Distinguishing Generals and Specifics*

What is general in one situation might be specific in another. Look at columns A and B and identify when the same word is specific and when it is general by writing the words *specific* and *general* on the blank line.

Exercise:

A. What is *Toyota* in A? ____________ in B? ____________

A.	B.
Toyota	Toyota
Pontiac	Celica
Cars	Corolla
Volkswagen	Corona

2. What is *cars* in A? ____________ in B? ____________

A.	B.
Cars	Transportation
Toyota	Boats
Pontiac	Cars
Volkswagen	Trains

3. What is *flower* in A? ____________ in B? ____________

A.	B.
Flower	Daisy
Tree	Flower
Bush	Rose
Vegetation	Lilac

INTRODUCTIONS

Focus: *Identifying Topics*

Cross out the item in each line which does not belong. Identify the *topic* of each group of items. See the example below.

Example:

	Topic
Monday; Tuesday; Wednesday; Thursday; Friday; ~~July~~	Days

Exercise:

1. A B C D 6 E F G.
2. Tokyo; Paris; Seoul; Riyadh; Madrid;
3. b c d f g h j k l m n o p q r s t v w x y z.
4. In the morning; in the afternoon; in the store; in the evening; at night.
5. Friendly; sad; happy; timid; skinny.
6. Indian; pig; bit; kite; hid.
7. He walks; we write; you study; they work; she listened.

Focus: *Identifying Topics in Paragraphs*

Read the following paragraphs and identify the *topic,* or what the paragraph is about, in one word. First look at the example.

Example:

Stamp-collecting is my sister's hobby. She collects old stamps and from different countries. I can always make my sister happy by giving her stamps for a present. Her stamps may be valuable in the future.

The **topic** of this paragraph is ______*stamps*______.

Now, read the following paragraphs and identify the topic in just one word.

Exercise:

Caroline has so many clothes that she can't put them in her closet anymore. She has a jogging suit, ten pairs of pants, twenty sweaters, five pairs of boots, twelve bathing suits, a coat, two jackets, and hundreds of hats and gloves.

The **topic** of this paragraph is ____________________.

There are different animals in the world. They are wild and domestic. Certain wild animals, such as lions, tigers, and apes, live in the jungle. Others, like polar bears, penguins, and reindeer, live in cold climates. Most domestic animals live with people in their homes. Dogs and cats are good examples of this.

The **topic** of this paragraph is ____________________.

Focus: *Writing Topic Sentences*

The topic of a paragraph is found in the *topic sentence.* It is in the paragraph, usually at the beginning, but not always. Topic sentences are umbrella sentences. This is because all other sentences come under the idea of the topic sentence. Read the following paragraphs and write complete topic sentences for them. First look at the example.

Example:

The most expensive gem is the diamond because it is rare and difficult to find. Another beautiful stone is the sapphire. It is blue. Emeralds are green and rubies are red. Opals are also nice stones.

Topic Sentence: *There are many kinds of precious stones*.

Now, read the following paragraphs and write the topic sentence on the line provided.

Exercise:

The most beautiful flowers are roses because they come in so many colors. Wild daisies are other beautiful flowers. Tulips, daffodils, and crocuses are pretty spring flowers.

Topic Sentence: ____.

Skiing is a pleasant sport for cold weather. Some people enjoy snowshoeing. Others like to go ice-skating. In the winter, my favorite sport is sledding.

Topic Sentence: ____.

Focus: ***Introductions and Topic Sentences***

When you meet people for the first time, you want to make an *impression* on them. In other words, you want to tell them something *interesting* in order to get their attention. If you do this, they will remember you and want to know more about you. The same is true for writing. In much the same way that boring people lose the attention of their listeners, so does boring writing. If the topic and introduction are not interesting, the reader won't want to continue. Facts are interesting and focus your audience on the topic. On the following lines, brainstorm things about yourself that you like to tell people when you meet them. Remember not to say, *"I'm going to tell you . . ."* Would you ever say to a person you were meeting for the first time, "I'm going to tell you my name. My name is . . . "? Well, you shouldn't do that when you write either.

Exercise:

______________________________ ______________________________
______________________________ ______________________________
______________________________ ______________________________
______________________________ ______________________________
______________________________ ______________________________

Focus: ***Interesting Introductions***

Read the following *introductions* and put a circle around the ones you think are most *interesting*. Think about why they are interesting and why they make good topic sentences.

Exercise:

1. When I was born they gave me a name.
2. My name is ________, and I'm a foreign student studying in the United States.
3. I live here, and I do homework.

1. I like my country, and you will too.
2. My country is nice and beautiful.
3. My country is a great place to visit because it has art, culture, and history.

1. My face still becomes hot and red when I remember an embarrassing day I had.
2. My most embarrassing moment made me feel shy.
3. I was very embarrassed one day.

BODIES

Focus: *Different Orderings*

There is no single correct *order*. Orders differ from one topic to another. The same group of items can seem different, depending upon the topic. Order the following pairs of identical information in different ways according to what the topic requires.

Exercise:

I. **Furniture**	**For size:**	**For comfort:**
A. Chair	A. ______	A. ______
B. Bed	B. ______	B.______
C. Table	C. ______	C.______
II. **Occupations**	**For highest earnings:**	**For lowest earnings:**
A. Dentist	A. ______	A. ______
B. Accountant	B. ______	B. ______
C. Teacher	C. ______	C. ______
III. **Fruit**	**From most favorite to least:**	**From most expensive to least:**
A. Apple	A. ______	A. ______
B. Orange	B. ______	B. ______
C. Banana	C. ______	C. ______
IV. **Family**	**From oldest to youngest:**	**From youngest to oldest:**
A. Sister	A. ______	A. ______
B. Mother	B. ______	B. ______
C. Father	C. ______	C. ______
V. **Army officers**	**From highest to lowest rank:**	**From lowest to highest rank:**
A. Colonel	A. ______	A. ______
B. General	B. ______	B. ______
C. Major	C. ______	C. ______
VI. **Important dates**	**From most recent to least recent:**	**From least recent to most recent:**
A. 1776	A. ______	A. ______
B. 1492	B. ______	B. ______
C. 1963	C. ______	C. ______

Focus:
Ordering Sentences

When writing, there are many possible orders. The topic sentence often comes first in a paragraph, but not always. There is not one correct order. However, some orders are more *logical* than others. Look at the following sentences and put in numbers which show *chronological* order. Then rearrange the sentences in paragraph form. Try to *begin* with a *topic* sentence and *end* with a *concluding* sentence.

Exercise:

__________ What do you want to do when you graduate (finish university)?

__________ When I graduate, I want to be a professor.

__________ There are so many things to teach that it would be easy to be a professor.

__________ Teaching is interesting.

__________ Besides, professors are happy, aren't they?

Focus:
Chronological Order

Exercise:

Assign the following pictures a correct *chronological (time) order* by using numbers.

__________ __________ __________

Focus:
Chronological Order Practice

Your teacher will assign you a partner to work with. Interview your partners about what they do in the evening. Then, write a paragraph about the answers you get from the following questions. Pay attention to *chronological order*.

Exercise:

1. When do you leave school every day? __________
2. What is the first thing you do? __________
3. After that, what do you do? __________

4. What time do you prepare dinner? ______________________________
____
5. When is it ready to eat? ______________________________
____
6. What do you usually eat for dinner? ______________________________
____
7. Where do you go when you finish dinner? ______________________________
____
8. What time do you go to bed? ______________________________
____
9. How many hours do you sleep? ______________________________
____
10. Do you dream? ______________________________
____

Exercise:

Now, write a paragraph in chronological order. Begin with a topic sentence which you indent at the X. Continue with the body and end with the conclusion.

Title: ______________________________

X ______________________________
____
____
____
____
____
____
____
____
____
____

Focus:
Spatial Order—
Prepositions

Look at the picture and fill in the missing *preposition* which describes the dog's *spatial relationship* to the chair and to the circle.

Lucas is ________ the chairs.

Lucas is ________ the chair.

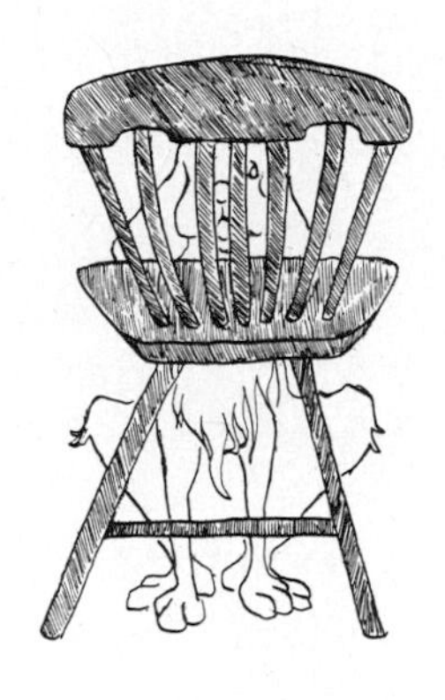

Lucas is ________ the chair.
Lucas is ________ the chair.

Lucas is ________ the chair.

Lucas is ________ the circle
Lucas is ________ the circle.

Lucas is ________ the circle.

Lucas is ________ the chair
Lucas is ________ the chair.

Lucas is ________ the chair.
Lucas is ________ the chair.

Focus:
Sticking to the Topic

You will learn to stay within the limits of your chosen topic by being able to decide which word is not included in the *umbrella* sentence. Every word is under the umbrella.

Exercise:

Which word is in the wrong group?

I. Cars
   A. Toyota
   B. Trans Am
   C. Bicycle

I. I like my apartment.
   A. Room
   B. Furniture
   C. Car

I. Animals
   A. Dog
   B. Flower
   C. Cat

I. My friend is happy.
   A. Sad
   B. Friendly
   C. Nice

I. Body
   A. Arm
   B. Leg
   C. Shoes

I. Vancouver is beautiful.
   A. Mountains
   B. Lakes
   C. Ugly

I. Food
   A. Hat
   B. Apple
   C. Hamburger

I. English is easy to learn.
   A. Difficult
   B. Speak
   C. Write

Focus:
Sticking to the Topic Practice

Good paragraphs should talk about one topic. Sometimes people forget and add another topic that doesn't go under the umbrella. Choose the sentences which don't belong in the paragraphs below. *Underline* one in each.

Example:

Summer is my favorite season. During the summer, there are many things I like to do—swimming, camping, waterskiing, sunbathing, and traveling. *My sister hates to go to the beach.* The best part about summer is that I am on vacation.

Exercise:

My mother is the nicest woman I know. All of my friends come to my house because they love to talk to mom. My best friend always tells mom about her problems. When there is a party, everyone invites my mother. I'm not very good at parties.

It is difficult to be a student. I wake up early for class every morning. My parents call me and write to me each week. I spend most of the day in class. Then I go home and do my homework. At night, I study for the next day's quiz.

CONCLUSIONS

Focus:
Concluding Sentences

People like things to end, or to be finished. We turn off the television; we close books; we wash dishes. These actions make us feel complete and satisfied. In like manner, writing needs to be finished. It is not good to write something that is incomplete. Good conclusions help make writing complete. They remind readers another time about the most important points in their reading. In other words, *conclusions* can summarize, restate the main ideas and topic, or come to a result. In short, they punctuate writing in much the same way that periods (.) punctuate sentences. In the following paragraph, think of three different conclusions that summarize, restate the main idea, and come to a result. You might want to work with your teacher or a partner. If you think that one of the three different conclusions doesn't apply, leave it blank.

Exercise:

Foreigners can practice English by reading magazines. People interested in news can read *Time* or *Newsweek*. These magazines give a general idea of the world situation. *National Geographic* and *Geo* don't discuss much news. However, they are good magazines for people who like nature. In addition to news and nature, there are magazines about clothing and fashion. *Vogue* is an example of this. ______________________________.

1. Conclusion that *summarizes:*

   ______________________________.

2. Conclusion that *restates the main idea:*

   ______________________________.

3. Conclusion that *comes to a result* or a *solution:*

   ______________________________.

REVIEW

Focus: *Generating Outlines*

In this practice, write sample outlines using one complete sentence for the introduction, one word for each specific idea in the body, and one complete sentence in the conclusion. The conclusion can be a *summary,* a *result,* or a *restatement.*

Exercise:

Title: My Apartment

Introduction: I. ______________________________.

A. ______________

Body: B. ______________

C. ______________

Conclusion: ______________________________

Title: My City

Introduction: I. ______________________________

A. ______________

Body: B. ______________

C. ______________

Conclusion: ______________________________

Title: Things I Have Not Done Yet

Introduction: I. ______________________________

A. ______________

Body: B. ______________

C. ______________

Conclusion: ______________________________

Focus: *Developing Outlines from Paragraphs*

An eight-sentence paragraph is presented here. Develop an outline on the basis of this composition. The introduction and conclusion in the outline are the same as those in the paragraph. You must find a concise word for the specific points in the body of the composition. The specific points have to be represented at least generally by the *topic* or *umbrella* in the introduction. Your teacher may want you to mention the points of grammar that are important on the line that says Grammar Focus.

Example:

Title: *Things I Have Not Done in San Francisco Yet*

1)There are many things I want to do that I have not done in San Francisco yet. 2)I have heard that the trolley cars are interesting to ride. 3)They travel up and down the hills of this lovely city. 4)I have read about the old section of San Francisco. 5)In addition to its physical beauty, Fisherman's Wharf has good places to listen to music. 6)I am probably the only person here who still has not visited the Golden Gate Bridge. 7)I plan to go there the next time I drive my car. 8)I hope to be able to see everything San Francisco has to offer before I return to my country.

Exercise:

Grammar Focus: ____________

Title: ____________

Introduction: I. ____________

A. ____________

Body: B. ____________

C. ____________

Conclusion: ____________

____

Focus: *Generating Sentences from Outlines*

Look at the outlines below. On a separate sheet of paper, develop *paragraphs* of about eight sentences based on the information provided in the outlines.

Exercise:

Title: My Country

Introduction: I. My country is an interesting place to visit.

A. People

Body: B. Food

C. Sights

Conclusion: People who visit my country can enjoy a variety of things.

Title: My Weekend

Introduction: I. I always try to enjoy my weekends by doing different activities.

A. Dancing

Body: B. Visiting

C. Playing

Conclusion: After a hard week, it is important to have fun on the weekend.

Focus:
Cloze Practice—Topics, Specifics, Conclusions

Fill in the missing parts of the outline based on your understanding of what good *organization* is. Remember what *topic sentences* and *conclusions* should do. Be specific in the *body* of your paragraph.

Exercise:

Title: How to Learn English

Introduction: I. ______________________________

Body:
A. Study
B. Speak
C. Read

Conclusion: ______________________________

Title: Why I have Chosen My Major

Introduction: I. There are several reasons why I have chosen my particular major.

Body:
A. ______________
B. ______________
C. ______________

Conclusion: I hope my major will help me to be useful in my country.

PRACTICE

Focus:
Cloze Practice—Developing the Paragraph Body

In the following example, the outline is completed, but sentences have been left out of the composition. Supply appropriate sentences to the paragraph based on your understanding of the outline.

Example:

Title: Studying in the United States

Introduction: I. There are many places to study English in the world, but I have good reasons for choosing the United States.

Body:
A. Pronunciation
B. Location
C. Education

Conclusion: I would rather learn English in the United States than in another English-speaking country.

Exercise:

Studying in the United States

[1]There are many places to study English in the world, but I have good reasons for choosing the United States. [2]First, I prefer the sound of American English to the sound of British English. [3]______________________________ ______________________________. [4]______________________________ ______________________________. [5]The United States is further from my country, so there are fewer chances for me to meet people who speak my native language. [6]Another reason to study English in the United States is the high quality of American language schools. [7]____ ______________________________. [8]In conclusion, I would rather learn English in the United States than in another English-speaking country.

2 Refining and Revising

CONNECTORS

In the previous chapter, you learned about different kinds of organization. You will see in this chapter that certain connectors are better suited for certain kinds of organization. You will review this idea later, when you learn about rhetorical devices.

Connectors, as the name suggests, are used to tie thoughts together. They connect words in a sentence and they connect ideas in a paragraph. As you become a better writer, you will want to express your ideas in a more complex way. When you write without connectors, you are limited to simple sentences. However, when you use connectors, you can write more complicated sentences. Instead of having sentences that seem unrelated like words on a supermarket shopping list, you will have sentences that show relationships to each other. You must be careful to use connectors correctly. Using them too much is just as bad as not using them enough. In addition, you need to know which connectors are appropriate for specific situations. Otherwise, your paragraph will be full of connectors that are sprinkled on the paper like salt on french fries.

Connectors bring life and variety to your writing. Without them, your writing can become boring. Now you are going to learn useful connectors and practice using them in some exercises. After you learn them, try to use them in your writing. You will create better compositions.

Focus: *List of Connectors*

Connectors tie thoughts together. They can join two separate sentences. When this is the case, use a period (.) for punctuation at the end of the first sentence. Because the connector begins a new sentence, it is capitalized and followed by a comma (,). Connectors are also used to join two phrases in one sentence. When this is the case, put a semicolon (;) after the first phrase and the connector after the semicolon. Do not capitalize the connector and put a comma after it. In the following chart, an asterisk (*) indicates the connectors which can have both kinds of punctuation. The two ways are shown in the following examples.

Examples:

He never studies. *T*herefore, he receives bad grades.
He never studies; *t*herefore, he receives bad grades.

Showing Addition	***Showing Results***	***Showing Opposition***	***Showing Examples***	***Showing Similarity***
and also *in addition *besides that *furthermore *moreover another reason *what is more *not only that *on top of that	so *consequently *hence then *therefore thus *as a result *for this/that reason *accordingly because of because since	but on the contrary yet *however *nevertheless on the other hand in contrast conversely otherwise although while	*for example *for instance such as one example of this is as an illus- tration take the case of e.g.	and in like manner in the same way likewise similarly
Showing Summary	***Showing Time***	***Showing Chronological Sequence***	***Showing Physical Relationship***	***Showing Emphasis***
in conclusion to summarize to conclude in short	when while before after since until as once ago anymore still yet	*first *second *third *then *next *later *finally	around near next to beside on top of, above in front of behind, in back of at the right at the left under, beneath	*indeed *in other words *in fact i.e.

Focus: *Connectors in Context*

The following sentences use the connectors above in context. You should try to use these connectors in your writing.

Showing Addition

And	I play soccer every Sunday *and* so does my husband.
Also	Today we studied grammar. We *also* studied spelling.
In addition	My brother has a store in New York; *in addition,* he is an insurance salesman.
Besides that	My mother can speak French very well. *Besides that,* she speaks German fluently.
Furthermore	She just wrote a book. *Furthermore,* she is writing a magazine article.
Moreover	They cut my hair too short. *Moreover,* they charged me $50!
Another reason	One reason she is crying is that she is homesick. *Another reason* is that she lost her wallet.
What is more	She is a well-known singer; *what's more,* she plays many instruments.
Not only that	U.C.L.A. is one of the best universities in California. *Not only that,* it is one of the most famous in the United States.

On top of that	They raised the prices at my favorite restaurant. *On top of that,* they made the portions smaller.

Showing Results

So	Bruce Springsteen is known for his great concerts. *So* if you want to see an American rock concert, you should get tickets to see this musician.
Consequently	They sat in the sun for a long time; *consequently,* they got sunburned.
Hence	The DC-10 is a comfortable and fast plane; *hence,* it is used by many companies.
Then	He doesn't like being single. *Then,* he should get married.
Therefore	He didn't make a plane reservation in advance; *therefore,* he couldn't get a seat in the non-smoking section.
Thus	He watches television all the time, *thus* he practices listening comprehension.
As a result	She got a high score on the TOEFL exam. *As a result,* she was accepted to a university.
For this/that reason	We aren't doing well in class; *for that reason,* we will probably need to take it again.
Accordingly	It is difficult to learn a new language; *accordingly,* I have to study six hours every day.
Because	It is good to study in an English-speaking country *because* you can practice English every day.
Because of	The game was cancelled *because of* the rain.
Since	You had better find a roommate *since* you don't like to live alone.

Showing Opposition

But	They produce oil in Kuwait, *but* they don't grow many vegetables.
On the contrary	She doesn't hate animals. *On the contrary,* she will not even eat animal meat.
Yet	He is a happy man, *yet* he never smiles.
However	I felt sick this morning; *however,* I went to work.
Nevertheless	Fast foods are bad for the health. *Nevertheless,* people often eat them.
On the other hand	You love to go to restaurants. *On the other hand,* you don't have a lot of money.
In contrast	The movie is violent. *In contrast,* its music is peaceful and romantic.
Conversely	Daylight lasts all summer in the North Pole. *Conversely,* nightfall lasts all winter.
Otherwise	If the students do well in English, they can begin their university studies. *Otherwise,* they have to study English for a longer time.
Although	*Although* I feel homesick, I can't call my parents every night.
Though	*Though* he is hungry at 7 A.M., he doesn't have time for breakfast.
While	*While* some people are happy, others are sad.

Showing Examples

For example	We traveled to many places; *for example,* we visited Japan, Egypt, Mexico and India.

For instance	More women have political positions now than ever before. *For instance,* the Democrats had a woman vice-presidential candidate in 1984.
Such as	Vegetables, *such as* broccoli, carrots and cauliflower, are good for your health.
One example of this is	There are many problems in poor countries. *One example of this is* starving children.
As an illustration	Ethiopia serves *as an illustration* of starvation in Africa.
Take the case of	Some countries that were enemies in the past have become friends. *Take the case of* Japan and the United States.
e.g.	Many foreign cars are used in the United States, *e.g.,* Toyota, Porsche, Volkswagen, and Fiat.

Showing Similarity

In like manner	When you live in another country, you should try to learn the language of that country. *In like manner,* when other people visit your country, they should try to speak your language.
In the same way	The United States boycotted the 1980 Olympics. *In the same way,* the U.S.S.R. didn't send their athletes to the 1984 Olympics.
Likewise	Students must follow the rules of the classroom. *Likewise,* people have to obey the laws of society.
Similarly	The train goes to Washington, D.C. regularly. *Similarly,* the Greyhound bus goes to Chicago every day.

Showing Summary

In conclusion	*In conclusion,* I am lucky to study here because it's a new and different experience.
To summarize	*To summarize,* three reasons to visit other countries are the culture, the language, and the people.
To conclude	*To conclude,* I am happy to be your president for the next four years.
In short	*In short,* the party was a big success, and everyone had a wonderful time.

Showing Time

When	*When* I arrived in the United States, my friend met me at the airport.
While	*While* she was taking a shower, the telephone rang.
Before	*Before* the party, we cleaned the house.
After	The house was dirty *after* the party.
Since	My husband and I have lived here *since* September.
Until	I am not going to open my presents *until* six o'clock.
As	The bell rang *as* the students arrived.
Once	*Once* the teacher explained the lesson, everything became clear.
Ago	I visited Spain six years *ago.*
Anymore	I don't smoke cigarettes *anymore.* I quit.
Still	After all these years, I *still* like the music of the 60s.
Yet	He hasn't seen that movie *yet.*

Showing Chronological Sequence

First	*First,* they went to the post office.
Second	*Second,* they went to the supermarket.
Third	*Third,* they brought their groceries home.

Then	*Then,* they walked to the library.
Later	*Later,* they went out for coffee.
Finally	*Finally,* they returned to their home.

Showing Physical Relationship

Around	There is a cafe *around* the corner.
Near	The bookstore is *near* the cafe.
Next to	*Next to* the bookstore, there is a great restaurant.
Beside	*Beside* the restaurant is a bank.
On top of	*On top of* the bank there is a chimney.
In front of	There are mailboxes and a money machine *in front of* the bank.
Behind	*Behind* the bank is a parking lot.
At the right	*At the right* of the parking lot is a gas station.
At the left	*At the left* of the gas station is the parking lot.
Under	The subway runs *under* the bookstore, restaurant, and bank.

Showing Emphasis

Indeed	Indira Gandhi was a famous Indian leader. *Indeed,* she will be missed and remembered by her people.
In other words	We are learning cursive writing; *in other words,* connected writing which is different from printing.
In fact	She is intelligent. *In fact,* she received a scholarship from her country.
i.e.	They are traveling through the New England states, *i.e.,* Maine, Massachusetts, Vermont, New Hampshire, Rhode Island and Connecticut.

Focus: *Showing Continuation of the Same Idea—Connectors of Addition*

Your writing needs to be smooth, not unconnected. You don't want it to sound like a list of things you need to buy at the supermarket. The following is a typical supermarket list.

I went to the store and bought:

bread	fruit
butter	vegetables
eggs	rice
cheese	milk
yogurt	flour

If you write about these items, you need to *connect* them in some way. You don't want to have lists in a composition. This can be avoided with the following *connectors of addition* which are used when listing items or connecting the same idea.

and, in addition, what is more, on top of that, furthermore, moreover, not only that, besides that, also

Example:

The other day I went to the store. I bought dairy products such as butter, eggs, cheese, yogurt, *and* milk. I *also* bought produce. *In addition,* I got some bread, rice, *and* flour. *Besides that,* I needed paper towels.

Exercise:

Now, brainstorm a list of items you can buy at the following three locations:

In a bookstore	***In a department store***	***In a farmer's market***
____________	____________	____________
____________	____________	____________
____________	____________	____________
____________	____________	____________

Then, on another sheet of paper, connect the ideas you have brainstormed with connectors of addition like the examples given above.

Focus: *Showing Cause and Effect Relationships—Connectors of Result*

Look at the examples of *cause and result* relationships given here. Think about how one thing makes the other thing happen.

Examples:

joking → laughter
rain → growth
hunger → eating
travel → homesickness
full tank → go far
study hard → pass exam

Exercise:

Now, see if you can brainstorm as many *cause and effect relationships* as you can think of.

__________ → __________ __________ → __________
__________ → __________ __________ → __________
__________ → __________ __________ → __________

Then choose at least five of the cause and effect words you have brainstormed and write sentences showing their relationship. The following *connectors of result* will help you. See the examples below.

so, therefore, consequently, as a result, for these reasons

Examples:

He always tells *jokes, so* she *laughs* a lot.

We *studied hard; therefore,* we *passed* the course.

We *traveled* to another country. *As a result,* he felt *homesick.*

Exercise:

Now, on another sheet of paper, try to connect the ideas from your brainstorm list with complete sentences.

Focus: *Showing Opposition— Connectors of Contrast*

First, brainstorm as many pairs of *opposites* as you can. Then decide if they are *adjectives, nouns,* or *verbs,* and organize them that way. Look at the examples.

Examples:

up—down	fast—slow	sleep—wake up
day—night	run—walk	land—sea
ugly—handsome	north—south	near—far
hate—love	black—white	

Classify them into adjectives*, nouns, verbs, etc. Very simply, adjectives describe nouns (persons, places, things), and verbs show actions.

Adjectives	***Nouns***	***Verbs***
black—white	hate—love	hate—love
north—south	day—night	sleep—wake up
ugly—handsome	land—sea	run—walk

In this space, brainstorm different pairs of *opposites:*

Exercise:

________—________	________—________	________—________
________—________	________—________	________—________
________—________	________—________	________—________

Look at your pairs of opposites and classify them into adjectives, nouns, and verbs, etc.

Exercise:

Adjectives	***Nouns***	***Verbs***
________—________	________—________	________—________
________—________	________—________	________—________
________—________	________—________	________—________

Exercise:

On another sheet of paper, write at least five sentences which show the contrary nature of the words you have brainstormed. The following *connectors of contrast* will help you. See the examples below before you do your own.

> but, however, nevertheless, on the contrary, in contrast, on the other hand

Examples:

She says she likes *handsome* boys, *but* her boyfriend is *ugly.*

We *love* our English teacher. *However,* we *hate* English.

He works all *night. On the contrary,* she works all *day.*

**See Appendix H for a complete list of adjectives and Appendix F for more practice in identifying parts of speech.*

Focus: *Showing Examples—Connectors of Exemplification and Classification*

Examples are used to develop ideas and give clarity to sentences. They also help *classify* things into groups. They paint a clear picture for the reader. Look at the differences between the two sentences given in the example.

Examples:

1. There are many *interesting places* to visit in New York.
2. The *Empire State Building,* the *United Nations,* the *Statue of Liberty,* and the *World Trade Center,* for example, are interesting places to visit in New York.

Notice that the second sentence gives the reader a lot more information.

Exercise:

Now, brainstorm lists of examples for the following topics:

Foods to eat in my country:	***My favorite hobbies:***	***Types of people I like:***
____________	____________	____________
____________	____________	____________
____________	____________	____________
____________	____________	____________

School subjects I don't like:	***Languages to learn:***	***Countries to visit:***
____________	____________	____________
____________	____________	____________
____________	____________	____________
____________	____________	____________

Try to write sentences using words which signal *examples* like the following:

> for example, for instance, such as, one example of this is, is an example of, e.g.

Examples:

1. There are many interesting places to visit in New York, *such as* the Empire State Building, the United Nations, the World Trade Center, and the Statue of Liberty.
2. There are different restaurants in Seattle. *For example,* there are fast food places, family restaurants, and ethnic restaurants.
3. That store only sells expensive cars. *For instance,* they have Porsches, Mercedes, Jaguars, and Rolls Royces, but they do not have used Volkswagens.

Exercise:

Now, from the list you have brainstormed above, use a separate sheet of paper and try to write sentences which use connectors that show examples. Look at the box if you need help.

Focus:
Showing Similarity—Connectors of Comparison

First, brainstorm pairs of words which have the *same* or *almost the same meaning*. Then, decide if they are adjectives, nouns or verbs and classify them that way. Look at the examples.

Examples:

run—jog	handsome—good-looking	nice—friendly
talk—speak	sea—ocean	car—automobile

Classify the above list into adjectives, nouns, and verbs.

Adjectives	***Nouns***	***Verbs***
handsome—good-looking	sea—ocean	run—jog
sad—unhappy	car—automobile	talk—speak

In these lines, brainstorm different pairs of words which have the *same* or *almost the same meaning:*

Exercise:

________—________	________—________	________—________
________—________	________—________	________—________
________—________	________—________	________—________

Exercise:

Look at your pairs of words and classify them into adjectives, nouns, verbs, etc.

Adjectives	***Nouns***	***Verbs***
________—________	________—________	________—________
________—________	________—________	________—________
________—________	________—________	________—________

Exercise:

Now, on another sheet of paper, write at least three sentences that show the similar nature of the words you have brainstormed. The following *connectors of comparison* will help you. Look at the examples which follow before you do your own.

similarly, likewise, in the same way, in like manner

Examples:

She only likes *handsome* men. *Similarly,* her brother only goes out with *good-looking* women.

They enjoy *running. In like manner,* we enjoy *jogging.*

The *ocean* is vast and mysterious. *Likewise,* the *sea* is immense and undiscovered.

Exercise:

Now, look at your brainstorm list. On a sheet of paper, write sentences that show comparison by finding the similarity in your ideas.

Focus: *Showing Summary—Connectors of Conclusion*

Look at the following paragraphs. Notice how they do not have concluding sentences. You can end these paragraphs by *summarizing, restating the main idea, or reaching a result or solution.* A good way to do that is by using *connectors which signal summary* like those in the box below. Remember that different kinds of writing require different kinds of conclusions.

in conclusion, to summarize, to conclude, in short

In the following paragraphs, add a suitable *conclusion* using the above connectors.

Exercise:

I go swimming at the neighborhood swimming pool five times a week. I love to swim for one hour and to feel the silence of the water. It is a relaxing sport. In addition to relaxation, I like to swim because it keeps me in shape. In other words, swimming makes me feel healthy. Furthermore, swimming is enjoyable because I can do it alone. If my friends are busy, I can go to the pool by myself.____.

I like to go to parties in order to celebrate special occasions. For example, birthdays are wonderful celebrations because people feel important on that day. On their birthdays, people receive presents and cards. Similarly, anniversaries are pleasant celebrations. They are a time for family and friends to congratulate a happily married couple. In addition, I enjoy weddings. It is nice to know that two people in love are going to spend their lives together. ____.

Focus: *Showing Time—Connectors of Temporal Relationships*

Look at the information about Bozo the Clown in the following time line chart. Pay careful attention to the *time relationships.** Then read the sentences about Bozo. Be sure to notice the *connectors which signal time,* like the ones in the box below. Then, write a similar time line about your own life and use the same connectors of time. Try to include information about your life in your country and your life here.

when, while, before, after, since, until, as, once, ago, anymore, still, yet

**See Appendix L for additional help with time words.*

Example:

BOZO's Time Line

Before 1980	***1981***	***After 1982***
Home: Los Angeles **Food:** Ice cream, cake, and chocolate milk **Transportation:** Tricycle **Clothing:** Colorful pants, big shoes **Feelings:** Happy and silly **Marital Status:** Single **Hobbies:** Telling jokes **Appearance:** Orange, curly hair **Profession:** Clown **Vices:** Chocolate	**Bozo decides to change his lifestyle**	**Home:** Vermont **Food:** Rice, vegetables, and juice **Transportation:** Bicycle and feet **Clothing:** Jeans and sandals **Feelings:** Serious and thoughtful **Marital Status:** Married **Hobbies:** Practicing yoga, reading, and writing **Appearance:** Short hair and beard **Profession:** Professor **Vices:** Pipes

When Bozo lived in Los Angeles, he ate ice cream and cake.
Bozo has lived in Vermont *since* 1982.
Until he moved to Vermont, Bozo rode a tricycle.
While he was telling jokes, Bozo felt happy and silly.
Bozo ate chocolate *before* he smoked pipes.
Once he changed his lifestyle, Bozo got married.
Bozo became a professor *after* he was a clown.
As he became serious, he began to read and write more.
He doesn't eat chocolate *anymore.*
He *still* doesn't drive.
He lived in L.A. some years *ago.*
He hasn't had a baby *yet.*

Following the example about Bozo's life, fill in the time line chart about *your* own life. Write sentences below using all the appropriate time signals.

Exercise:

My Life

Before 19__		***After 19__***
Home: **Food:** **Transportation:** **Clothing:** **Feelings:** **Marital Status:** **Hobbies:** **Appearance:** **Profession:** **Vices:**	**I decided to change my life and come here.**	**Home:** **Food:** **Transportation:** **Clothing:** **Feelings:** **Marital Status:** **Hobbies:** **Appearance:** **Profession:** **Vices:**

Sentences:

when ______________________________

while ______________________________

before ______________________________

after ______________________________

since ______________________________

until ______________________________

as ______________________________

once ______________________________

ago ______________________________

anymore ______________________________

still ______________________________

yet ______________________________

Focus: *Showing Chronological Sequence— Connectors of Time Order*

Look at the following sentences. They are out of order. Arrange them in chronological (time) order with the use of numbers. Then, replace the numbers with *signal words which show chronological order,* and write the sentences in a paragraph. The following chronological connectors will help you.

first, second, after, later, next, at last, finally

Exercise:

Numbers

__________ I came home after school.

__________ I woke up early in the morning.

__________ I cooked dinner.

__________ I went to my morning class.

__________ I slept for eight hours when I got home from work.

__________ I taught my evening class.

__________ I ate lunch.

Using a separate sheet of paper, arrange the above sentences in a paragraph and use *time words* in place of numbers. Begin with the word "first."

Focus: *Showing Physical Relationships— Connectors of Spatial Order*

Look at the picture below and describe where everything is in relation to the dog. Use *connectors* which show *spatial relationships* like those in the box.

around, near, next to, beside, in front of, behind, by, at the right, at the left, under

Exercise:

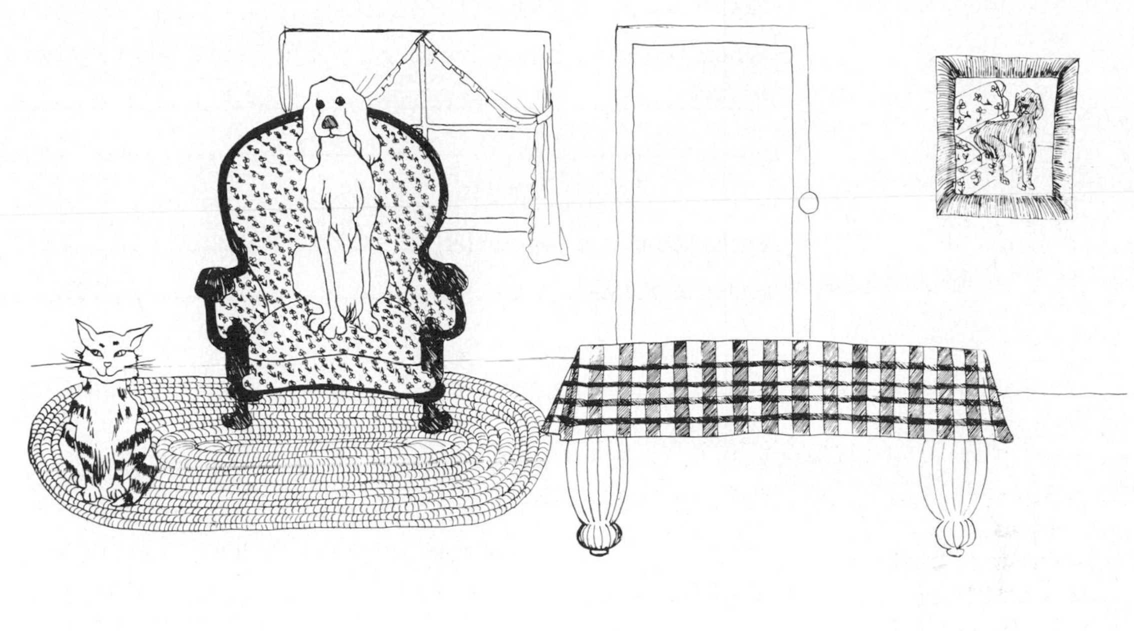

________________________________ the dog is a window.

________________________________ the dog's chair is a rug.

________________________________ the dog is a chair.

________________________________ the dog is a door.

________________________________ the dog is a table.

________________________________ the dog is a cat.

Now, on a separate sheet of paper, write the above sentences in paragraph form instead of list form.

Focus: *Showing Emphasis— Connectors of Iteration*

Sometimes it is necessary to make yourself very clear. If you are saying something important, you need to make sure that your reader understands what you are saying. One way to do this is by *repeating* yourself. Another way is by *saying the same thing* in a different way. A third way might be by *summarizing* in a short way what you said in more detail before. These are all forms of *iteration*. Iteration clarifies what you are saying. It also places *stress* or *emphasis* on important things. The examples in the box are connectors of iteration. Look at them before you read the following sentences. Then *emphasize* the important parts of what you read by adding a sentence that begins with a connector of iteration. First see the example.

indeed, in other words, in fact, i.e.

Example:

While you are living in another country, you must obey the laws of that country. *In other words, you cannot speed, steal, drink and drive, or break any laws.*

Which idea is emphasized above? *Must obey the laws.*

Exercise:

Now you try it. Make sure to circle what it is you have emphasized or tried to make clear before you add a sentence which begins with a connector of iteration.

When you learn a new language, you have to study very hard and very often. *In fact,* ____

____

My teacher is a vegetarian. *In other words,* ____

____

John Lennon, the famous ex-Beatle, was killed in front of his own apartment. *Indeed,* ____

____

She loves different kinds of animals, e.g., dogs, horses and cats. *In fact,* ____

____

Focus: ***Connectors in Context***

Look at the following paragraphs and decide if they are illustrations of *addition, contrast, result,* or *example.* Write the type of relationship on the line above the paragraph. Then fill in the blanks with the correct connectors which show the relationships of *addition, contrast, result,* and *example.* You can avoid repeating yourself by varying your use of connectors. Look at the connectors on page 24.

Exercise:

____________________ **Type of paragraph**

1. On my last birthday, I had a party and all of my friends and family attended. I received many lovely gifts. My parents gave me a bracelet ________________ a sweater. ________________, they bought me a pair of boots. ________________, I got earrings from my sister and brother-in-law. My friends brought me books, a candle, and ________________ a hat. ________________, I received tickets to a play.

____________________ **Type of paragraph**

2. My cousin and I are completely different. I love dogs. ________________, she hates dogs and loves cats. I prefer cold weather. ________________, she likes hot, dry climates. In my free time, I always travel, ________________ she never does. ________________, she did take a trip last summer.

________________**Type of paragraph**

3. I had a bad day yesterday and nothing went right. In the morning my alarm clock didn't go off ________________ I didn't wake up at 8 A.M. ________________, I arrived late to class ________________ my teacher was angry. ________________, I must come to class early tomorrow.

________________**Type of paragraph**

4. I am a person with many opinions. I know what I like and what I don't like. ________________, I like sports. Tennis, horseback riding, swimming, and ice-skating are fun. I dislike pale colors, ________________ pink, yellow, and baby blue, but I like bright colors, ________________, red, blue, and purple. I don't enjoy scientific subjects. ________________ is chemistry. My favorite subjects are in the field of humanities, ________________, music, literature, and languages.

Focus: *Mixed Connectors*

Look at the following paragraphs and think about the relationships being expressed. Fill in the blanks with connectors which illustrate those relationships. There can be a mixture of connectors which show *addition, contrast, result,* or *example.*

Exercise:

1. Last weekend, I was going to do many things. ________________ I wanted to study, clean my house, and write letters. ________________, I didn't do any of those things. ________________, I visited friends, went to a movie, and ate at a restaurant. ________________, I felt bad on Monday because I didn't do my homework, my house was dirty, and I didn't write to my family. ________________, my teacher was angry, my roommates wouldn't talk to me, and my parents won't receive any mail from me.

   Use similar connectors for the following paragraph. In addition, use connectors of time like *first, next, later, finally.*

2. Last week an old man went to the doctor. ________________, the doctor told him that he must go on a diet because he was too fat, and this was bad for the heart. ________________, the old man promised to listen to the doctor's advice. ________________, when the man left the office, he passed McDonald's and ate a lot of food. ________________, he had a hamburger, french fries, a coke, and some apple pie. ________________, he had ice cream. When he got home, he had three beers, chicken, and rice. ________________, he had a heart attack and died the next morning.

Add connectors to the following paragraph.

3. The prisoner was released (freed) from prison ________________ his good behavior. ________________, he did many bad things immediately. ________________, in one week he stole three cars and robbed ten banks. ________________, he had fights with fifteen people! ________________, he is in prison again.

RHETORICAL DEVICES AND ORGANIZATIONAL STRATEGIES

Just as connectors are suitable for specific situations, different kinds of writing are used for different purposes. All writing situations are not alike, and each type has different requirements. Therefore, you need to understand which type or pattern of writing is most appropriate for the situation. The purpose of your writing will determine the pattern. For example, if you want to give the details of a story so that the reader can *see* what you mean, you use *description*. If you want to break a story into its parts, you can use *classification* or *exemplification*. If you want to explain the steps of how to do something, you use *process*. If you give the reasons or results of something you do, you might use *cause and effect*. Or, if you are discussing the similarities and differences of a subject, *comparison and contrast* is a good device. What is more, if you want to make something very clear to your readers, you might save them a trip to the dictionary by using *definition*. These are some ways of organizing and can be used either by themselves or by combining them with other kinds. It is possible to have a purely descriptive composition. On the other hand, you might want to include comparison and contrast as part of your description. This is for you to decide. You might want to discuss your ideas with your teacher.

In this section, some different ways of talking about a subject, commonly known as *rhetorical devices,* are presented. Your teacher will guide you through the exercises and examples to help you understand these different patterns of organization. Then, include them in your own work. Try to combine these ideas with the connectors you have practiced in the previous section. They work well together. You will see similarities among ordering the body of the paragraph, using connectors, and organizing with rhetorical devices. After you study each type of organization, you might want to look at Chapters 3 and 4 to study a model of the rhetorical devices you have learned in Chapter 2.

Focus: ***Brainstorming Composition Topics—Rhetorical Devices***

On page 1 you brainstormed a list of composition topics. Now, think of more topics that you might want to write about. The following is an incomplete brainstorm list. You can complete it with topics that interest you.

Exercise:

Books ______________________

Houses ______________________

Cats ______________________

Homesickness ______________________

Mountains ______________________

Cars ______________________

Family ______________________

Peace ______________________

Focus: ***Brainstorming Questions Rhetorical Devices***

There are many different ways you can talk about a topic. One way of doing this is by asking yourself all the possible *questions* that come to your mind about that topic. In this exercise, imagine that you are going to write about *your family*. Brainstorm all the different questions you can about your family. It's best to limit yourself to *WH* and *H* questions like *Who?, What?, How?,* etc. If you need to practice questions, see the *WH?* exercises on pages 40–42.

Exercise:

Questions

______________________________ ______________________________

______________________________ ______________________________

______________________________ ______________________________

______________________________ ______________________________

______________________________ ______________________________

____

Focus: *WH and H Question Practice*

Write the *WH* and *H* questions that correspond to the underlined words. Be sure that your questions can be answered by the underlined words.

Exercise:

1. Stewart (A) reads his (B) book (his book = C) in the library (D) every day (E).

A. ______________________________?

B. ______________________________?

C. ______________________________?

D. ______________________________?

E. ______________________________?

2. Candace (A) is driving (B) a fast car (C) on the freeway (D) right now (E) because she is in a hurry to see her daughter (F).

A. ______________________________?

B. ______________________________?

C. ______________________________?

D. ______________________________?

E. ______________________________?

F. ______________________________?

Focus: *WH and H Question Practice*

Exercise:
Write the *WH* and *H* questions that correspond to the underlined words. Follow the previous exercise.

1. Natalie (A) often (B) plays with her (C) dog in the park (D).

A. ______________________________?

B. ______________________________?

C. ______________________________?

D. ______________________________?

2. A <u>beautiful</u> girl is buying <u>a lot</u> <u>of food</u> in the supermarket <u>now</u>.
   (A: beautiful; B: a lot; C: of food; D: now)

A. ______________________________?

B. ______________________________?

C. ______________________________?

D. ______________________________?

3. The <u>good</u> students <u>practiced</u> <u>some</u> <u>difficult</u> exercises <u>at home</u> <u>yesterday</u> <u>in order to learn English</u>.
   (A: good; B: practiced; C: some; D: difficult; E: at home; F: yesterday; G: in order to learn English)

A. ______________________________?

B. ______________________________?

C. ______________________________?

D. ______________________________?

E. ______________________________?

F. ______________________________?

G. ______________________________?

Focus:
WH and H Question Practice

Exercise:
Write the *WH* and *H* questions that correspond to the underlined words as you did in the preceding exercises.

1. <u>Vanessa and Tara</u> listen to <u>Lori</u> <u>attentively</u>.
   (A: Vanessa and Tara; B: Lori; C: attentively)

A. ______________________________?

B. ______________________________?

C. ______________________________?

2. <u>Grandma</u> is waiting for <u>the bus</u> at <u>the corner</u>.
   (A: Grandma; B: the bus; C: the corner)

A. ______________________________?

B. ______________________________?

C. ______________________________?

3. <u>Joe</u> looks at <u>Takako</u> often <u>because he's in love with her</u>.
   (A: Joe; B: Takako; C: because he's in love with her)

A. ______________________________?

B. ______________________________?

C. ______________________________?

4. <u>Diane</u> can't wait for <u>Hans</u> <u>because she's sick</u>.
   (A: Diane; B: Hans; C: because she's sick)

A. ______________________________?

B. ______________________________?

C. ______________________________?

5. Jay had to open it with a can opener.
(A = Jay; B = it; C = with a can opener)

A. ____?

B. ____?

C. ____?

6. We should get out of the taxi.
(A = taxi)

A. ____?

7. They persuaded Clancy to play five songs for them on the guitar.
(A = They; B = Clancy; C = five; D = them)

A. ____?

B. ____?

C. ____?

D. ____?

8. You like to travel by Greyhound bus.
(A = You; B = Greyhound; C = by Greyhound bus)

A. ____?

B. ____?

C. ____?

9. Ann might not wait for the mail carrier.
(A = mail carrier)

A. ____?

Focus: *Different Ways to See the Same Thing*

From the list you made on page 39, look at the word *books*. The following examples show six different ways to talk about *books* as a topic. After looking at the *books* example, use another sheet of paper to write about the word *family* in six ways. If you have other ideas about how to discuss this topic, please add them. Notice how it helps to ask yourself questions when you want to look at one subject in different ways.

Examples:

BOOKS

For example?	**Classification and Exemplification**	There are different categories of books. Some have hard covers and others have soft covers. Some are for studying and others are for free time. For school, grammar texts, encyclopedias and dictionaries are used. For pleasure, novels are read. For religious purposes, some people read the Bible, the Koran, the Torah, and other works.
How?	**Process**	It is not difficult to own a book. First, you go to the bookstore. Then, you find a book that you like. After that, you pay for the book at the cashier's desk. Then, you take it home. Later, you open the book. Next, you read it. Finally, you close the book and think about it.

What kind is it?	**Description**	A book is square or rectangle. It has a cover on the front and on the back. Sometimes the covers are hard and sometimes they are soft. Between the covers there are pages with information on them. The pages are often white and the words are black.
What is it like/unlike?	**Comparison and Contrast**	Books are like magazines and newspapers because you can read them. They are not like movies and music because you don't watch them or listen to them.
What is it?	**Definition**	A written or printed literary composition on consecutive sheets of paper bound together in a volume. A division of literary work.
Why?	**Cause and Effect**	There are good reasons to own books.

Focus: *Rhetorical Devices—Appropriate Questions*

On page 40 you made a list of questions. Now that you have practiced writing about topics in different ways, decide which *WH* and *H* questions you ask in order to discuss your topic in the following ways. Put the question on the blank line. You are given one answer as an example.

Example:

______*What kind is it*______? **Description**

Exercise:

______________________? **Definition**
______________________? **Comparison**
______________________? **Contrast**
______________________? **Classification/Exemplification**
______________________? **Process**
______________________? **Cause and Effect**

Focus: *Brainstorming—Classification and Exemplification of Different Points of View*

Think of one subject using all your senses. Use your eyes, your nose, your ears, your fingers, and your mouth. Brainstorm everything that comes to your mind. Look at the example to help you.

Example:

Subject: A Traditional Holiday in My Country (the United States)

Christmas

Look	***Taste***	***Sound***	***Smell***	***Feel***
red and green lights	sweets	presents	trees	cold outside
colorful	cakes	paper opening	cookies baking	warm inside
Santa Claus	turkey	voices	turkey roasting	exciting
snow falling	candy canes	music playing	candles burning	
tree decorations		family laughter	fresh	

Now think about a traditional holiday you like in your country, and brainstorm the things that come to your mind. Use your five senses.

Exercise:

Look	***Taste***	***Sound***	***Smell***	***Feel***
________	________	________	________	________
________	________	________	________	________
________	________	________	________	________
________	________	________	________	________
________	________	________	________	________
________	________	________	________	________

Focus:
Classifying Different Points of View in Outline Form

Take your brainstorm list from above and organize it in *outline form.* Look at the example first.

Example:

Title: A Traditional Holiday in My Country

I. Christmas is a traditional holiday in the United States.
   A. The way things look
   B. The way things taste
   C. The way things sound
   D. The way things smell
   E. The way things feel

Now, put *your* information in the same outline form. You can change the words if you like, to make them different from the example.

Exercise:

Title: ______________________________

I. ______________________________
   A. ______________________________
   B. ______________________________
   C. ______________________________
   D. ______________________________
   E. ______________________________

Focus:
Writing About Specifics

Look at your lists of A, B, C, D, E above and the ideas that came to your mind for the list above. *Circle* two ideas for each letter and then make them into complete sentences. Look at the example below before you do your own on a separate sheet of paper.

Example:

Subject: A Traditional Holiday in My Country

I. Christmas is a traditional holiday in the United States.
   A. The way things look—colorful lights, Santa Claus, snow falling, tree decorations

1. *Choose two:*
2. *Write one sentence for each:*

- Beautiful snow falls, and the world is white.
- Colorful lights hang on houses and shine on the white snow.

1. *Choose two:*
2. *Write one sentence for each:*

B. The way things taste—sweet, cakes, turkey, candy canes, sweet potatoes, drinks
- Fruit cakes are delicious and sweet.
- The hot chocolate tastes warm and creamy.

1. *Choose two:*
2. *Write one sentence for each:*

C. The way things sound—opening presents, voices, music playing, people's laughter
- I hear the sounds of presents being opened.
- People laugh and are happy about their gifts.

1. *Choose two:*
2. *Write one sentence for each:*

D. The way things smell—trees, kitchen smells, fresh
- The living room smells like evergreen trees.
- It is fresh and like outdoors inside.

1. *Choose two:*
2. *Write one sentence for each:*

E. The way things feel—cold outside, warm inside, exciting
- The snow makes everything cold outside.
- The Christmas feeling makes everything warm inside.

Focus: *Outline and Paragraph*

Choose three of the letters from A, B, C, D, E on page 44. First arrange them in outline form again. Then, put the sentences that you wrote for each letter in paragraph form. Don't worry about a conclusion now.

Example:

Title: My Favorite Holiday

I. Christmas is a traditional holiday in the United States.
   A. The way things look
   B. The way things sound
   C. The way things feel

Christmas is a traditional holiday in the United States. At that time, beautiful snow falls everywhere, and the world is white. Colorful lights hang on houses and shine on the white snow. In the house, I hear the sounds of presents being opened. People laugh and are happy about their gifts. Outside, the snow makes everything cold. However, the Christmas feeling makes everything warm inside.

Write your outline first. Then on a separate sheet of paper, write your paragraph. Remember to leave a space at the beginning of your first sentence. Look at the example. This is called *indenting*.

Exercise:

Title: ______________________________

I. ______________________________
   A. ______________________________
   B. ______________________________
   C. ______________________________

Focus: *Classifying Detail Through Questions*

First, look at the subject in the example. Then, in the following exercise, brainstorm ideas about that subject based on different *WH and H* questions. By doing this, you will develop more factual *details* for your topic. First look at the example, and then do the same thing for the topic, but relate it to your own personal experience.

Example:

Subject: Places a Person Should Visit in My City, New York

What?	*When?*	*Where?*	*How?*
Empire State Building	summer	midtown	by car
Statue of Liberty	spring	downtown	by ferry
Coney Island	autumn	Brooklyn	by subway
Fifth Avenue	morning	uptown	on foot
	during sales		

Exercise:

Subject: Places a Tourist Should Visit in My Country

For instance?	*What kind is it?*	*Why?*	*What is it like/unlike?*	*What is it?*
______	______	______	______	______
______	______	______	______	______
______	______	______	______	______
______	______	______	______	______
______	______	______	______	______

Focus:
Process—Brainstorming

From the following list of topics choose three and brainstorm every part of the *process*. Don't worry about correct order at this time. Just give the steps of the process. Then, add other things that you know how to do well.

Exercise:

How to use chopsticks:

____
____
____

How to make kapsa/enchiladas/sushi:

____
____
____

How to get a driver's license:

____
____
____

How to get a visa/passport:

____
____
____

How to learn a foreign language:

____
____
____

How to meet Americans in the United States:

____
____
____

Now, use another sheet of paper to brainstorm other processes that you can do well.

Focus:
Process—Chronological Order

Choose one of your brainstorm lists from the preceding exercise and put it in *chronological order* (time order) through the use of numbers. Make sure the steps of the process are in correct order.

Exercise:

How to ____________________

1. ____________________
2. ____________________
3. ____________________
4. ____________________
5. ____________________
6. ____________________

Now, replace the numbers with time signal words—*first, second, third, next, after that,* and *finally*. In the spaces provided below, write complete sentences with these words.

How to ____________________

First, ____________________

____

____

____

____

____

Focus:
Process—Chronological Order

You have seen that some words help you to know where a sentence goes in a paragraph. For example, the word *first* tells you the sentence goes at the beginning. Other words like *second, next,* and, *then* tell you about the information that comes after the beginning. At the end, you can see words like *finally, therefore, in short,* and *for these reasons.* Use numbers to put the sentences in order the way they are in a paragraph. First look at the example.

Example:

__5__ Finally, you eat breakfast.

__1__ First, you put the butter in the pan.

__3__ After that, you add the eggs and watch them fry.

__4__ Now, you take them out of the pan, and put them on the plate.

__2__ Next, you wait for the butter to melt.

Now, put in the numbers to show the correct order of these sentences.

Exercise:

_____ Then, you put the car in first gear.

_____ Next, you step on the clutch.

_____ Finally, you drive away.

_____ After that, you step on the gas and pull out.

_____ First, you turn on the car with a key.

Focus: *Process*

A *process* is another way to write about a topic. You use process writing to explain *how* you do something. Therefore, a process answers the question *How?* Since it is important to have *chronological time order* in a process, the following box of *chronological connectors* will be useful to you:

first, second, next, then, after that, later, finally

Look at the following examples of step-by-step process which are written as *lists* and not paragraphs.

Examples:

How to Braid Hair

1. Brush hair until smooth.
2. Separate into three sections.
3. Take first section in right hand and third section in left hand.
4. Put first section over second.
5. Place third section between first and second.
6. Repeat action until most of the hair is braided.
7. Tie remaining hair with band.

How to Drive a Standard Transmission

1. Turn on ignition, and step on gas.
2. Put left foot on clutch and right foot on brake.
3. Shift gear from neutral to first.
4. Slowly remove left foot from clutch.
5. Place right foot on gas pedal and accelerate.
6. Put left foot on clutch and shift to second, third, etc., depending on speed while removing right foot from gas.
7. Drive carefully.

Now look at the first list written in paragraph form with chronological connectors instead of numbers. Do the same for the second list.

Example:

How to Braid Hair

It is not difficult to braid hair. *First,* brush the hair until it becomes smooth. *Second,* separate it into three sections. *Then,* take the first section in your right hand and the third section in your left hand. *After that,* put the first section over the second. *Next,* place the third section between the first and second. *Then,* repeat the action until most of the hair is braided. *Finally,* tie the remaining hair with a band.

Exercise:

How to Drive a Standard Transmission

____
____
____
____
____
____
____
____
____
____
____
____
____

Now, think about something that you do very well. Write a chronological list of every step you do in the process. Next to the list, write a paragraph about the process. Replace the numbers with chronological connectors.

Exercise:

How to ______________________

1. ______________________
2. ______________________
3. ______________________
4. ______________________
5. ______________________
6. ______________________
7. ______________________

How to ______________________

____
____
____
____
____
____
____
____
____
____
____
____

Focus:
Description

Description is used to describe a topic. It is usually used with stories. Stories are also called *narratives*. Descriptions often answer the questions *What kind of?* and *Which?* For this reason, *adjectives** are usually used. Adjectives are words which describe things. To practice description, brainstorm words which describe *marriage*. Then describe the marriage customs in your country. Make sure to answer the questions that someone might ask you and to use connectors in your descriptive paragraph about marriage customs in your homeland. Perhaps the following *connectors of time* will be helpful.

when, while, before, after, since, until, as, once, ago, anymore, yet

Exercise:

Words which describe marriage:

Religious ____________ ____________

Expensive ____________ ____________

Beautiful ____________ ____________

Happy ____________ ____________

Exercise:

On another sheet of paper, write a *descriptive paragraph* titled *Marriage Customs in My Country.*

Focus:
Comparison and Contrast—Different Approaches to Organization

When you talk about two or more things, you can make your description clear by discussing the things they have in common and the things which they do not share. The *similarities,* the things in common, will express *comparison*. The *differences,* the things not in common, will express *contrast*. Here are two ways that you can talk about similarities and differences in an organized fashion. One way is to focus on each main subject individually. If you compare dogs and cats, for example, you first discuss all the information about dogs **(A)** as a block or unit and then compare and contrast all the information about cats **(B)**. This format is essentially **AAABBB.** Look at the following example.

Individual Main Subject Approach

Example:

I. Dogs
  A. Cost
    1. Original Investment
    2. Food
    3. Medical Bills
  B. Behavior
    1. Independence
    2. Sleeping
    3. Eating
  C. Style
    1. Breed
    2. Purpose
    3. Size

II. Cats
  A. Cost
    1. Original Investment
    2. Food
    3. Medical Bills
  B. Behavior
    1. Independence
    2. Sleeping
    3. Eating
  C. Style
    1. Breed
    2. Purpose
    3. Size

**A complete list of adjectives appears in Appendix H.*

The second way is to discuss the similarities and differences by combining the specific characteristics of each main subject. If you compare dogs and cats, you first discuss one point about dogs and then compare or contrast the same point about cats. You then return to dogs and back to cats in an alternating fashion. The format is essentially **ABABAB.** Look at the example.

Alternating Specific Characteristics Approach

Example:

I. Cost
 A. Dogs
  1. Original Investment
  2. Food
  3. Medical Bills
 B. Cats
  1. Original Investment
  2. Food
  3. Medical Bills

II. Behavior
 A. Dogs
  1. Independence
  2. Sleeping
  3. Eating
 B. Cats
  1. Independence
  2. Sleeping
  3. Eating

III. Style
 A. Dogs
  1. Breed
  2. Purpose
  3. Size
 B. Cats
  1. Breed
  2. Purpose
  3. Size

Focus:
Comparison and Contrast—Practice in Organization

Look at the information below about *Superman and Supergirl.*

	Superman	***Supergirl***
1. **Height:**	6 feet 3 inches	5 feet 8 inches
2. **Weight:**	200 pounds	120 pounds
3. **Age:**	35	30
4. **Intelligence:**	smart	brilliant
5. **Eye color:**	brown	green
6. **Hair:**	black	brown
7. **Favorite food:**	soup	salad
8. **Hobbies:**	flying	walking up buildings
9. **Looks:**	handsome	beautiful
10. **Personality:**	shy	assertive

Exercise:

Use the outline for Individual Main Subject Approach (page 50) and Alternating Characteristics Approach (page 51) as a guide, and try to classify this information. Do these outlines on a separate sheet of paper.

Focus:
Comparison and Contrast—Paragraph Practice

Now you are ready to write your comparison and contrast paragraphs based on these two kinds of organization. Remember to use *connectors* of *opposition* and *similarity* to tie your ideas together. The following box will be a reminder.

but, yet, however, nevertheless, on the other hand, in contrast, etc.
and, in like manner, in the same way, likewise, similarly, etc.

Exercise:

For practice, write two different organization style paragraphs about a comparison and contrast between Superman and Supergirl. Use another sheet of paper.

Focus:
Definition

Definition is another way to talk about a topic. Definitions are used to make ideas clear. They can also be used as introductions. This is common in academic writing, the kind you might do in your university classes. The best place to find a good definition is in the dictionary. However, if you write clear definitions, your reader will not have to use a dictionary to understand your meaning. Good definitions will clarify the idea for your reader. The best way to be clear is to use specific words, examples, and details. Don't use general adjectives like *nice* or general adverbs like *very*. Be as precise and direct as possible. To see an example, look up the word *love* in your dictionary and write down the definition. Make sure your definition answers the question, *What is it?*

Definition of love:

____

____

____

____

____

Now, can you extend the dictionary definition of love by adding your ideas of what it is and what it is not? Definitions also answer the question *What is it not?* The following connectors, which signal examples, might be helpful.

for example, for instance, such as, one example of this is, as an illustration, take the case of, e.g.

Exercise:

On a separate sheet of paper, try to write a definition of *What Love is and What It is Not*.

Focus:
Definition—Brainstorming and Practice

The following words are not English words. They are foreign words that come from your languages. However, they are used in English every day. From the following words, choose the ones that are familiar to you and brainstorm ideas about these words which will make their meanings or *definitions* clear.

Exercise:

Kimono	***Poncho***	***Chow mein***
____________	____________	____________
____________	____________	____________
____________	____________	____________
____________	____________	____________

Sputnik	***Alcohol***	***Kindergarten***
________	________	________
________	________	________
________	________	________
________	________	________

Sheik	***Chaise lounge***	***Shampoo***
________	________	________
________	________	________
________	________	________
________	________	________

Focus: ***Cause and Effect—Different Approaches to Organization and Practice***

Cause and effect is the last way of organizing writing in this chapter. This type of writing usually asks the question *Why?* and then answers it. Like comparison and contrast writing, there are two main ways to organize cause and effect compositions. One way is the group approach in which you talk first about all the causes together as a group and then about all the effects as a group. The pattern is **AAAAABBBBB.** The other way to organize this kind of writing is the alternating chain approach. In this case, first you discuss a cause and its effect, then another cause and its effect, etc. The pattern is **AB AB AB AB AB.** You will decide which type is better depending on your topic. If the relationship between cause and effect is difficult to see, you might prefer the group approach. On the other hand, if there is a direct relationship between cause and effect, the alternating chain approach might be better. In fact, you might want to combine both types at different times. First, look at the following composition topics. Next, in a *group approach,* brainstorm all the causes and then all the effects of those problems. Think about the *Why?* of the problem and the *result.* You might want to work in small groups for this exercise.

Exercise:

I. ***High Divorce Rate in the United States***
  A. Causes
    1.
    2.
    3.
    4.
    5.
  B. Effects
    1.
    2.
    3.
    4.
    5.

I. ***The Cold War***
  A. Causes
    1.
    2.
    3.
    4.
    5.
  B. Effects
    1.
    2.
    3.
    4.
    5.

I. ***Increased Interest in Health-Related Hobbies***
   A. Causes
      1.
      2.
      3.
      4.
      5.
   B. Effects
      1.
      2.
      3.
      4.
      5.

I. ***Drug Abuse by Teenagers***
   A. Causes
      1.
      2.
      3.
      4.
      5.
   B. Effects
      1.
      2.
      3.
      4.
      5.

I. ***The Women's Liberation Movement***
   A. Causes
      1.
      2.
      3.
      4.
      5.
   B. Effects
      1.
      2.
      3.
      4.
      5.

I. ***The Popularity of ________ Music***
   A. Causes
      1.
      2.
      3.
      4.
      5.
   B. Effects
      1.
      2.
      3.
      4.
      5.

I. ***High Suicide Rate Among Young People***
   A. Causes
      1.
      2.
      3.
      4.
      5.
   B. Effects
      1.
      2.
      3.
      4.
      5.

I. ***The Increased Use of Computers***
   A. Causes
      1.
      2.
      3.
      4.
      5.
   B. Effects
      1.
      2.
      3.
      4.
      5.

I. ***The Population Explosion***

A. Causes
1.
2.
3.
4.
5.

B. Effects
1.
2.
3.
4.
5.

I. ***Starvation in Third World Countries***

A. Causes
1.
2.
3.
4.
5.

B. Effects
1.
2.
3.
4.
5.

I. ***The Devaluation of ________ (Foreign Money)***

A. Causes
1.
2.
3.
4.
5.

B. Effects
1.
2.
3.
4.
5.

I. ***Illegal Aliens***

A. Causes
1.
2.
3.
4.
5.

B. Effects
1.
2.
3.
4.
5.

I. ***The Generation Gap***

A. Causes
1.
2.
3.
4.
5.

B. Effects
1.
2.
3.
4.
5.

I. ***Violence on the Screen***

A. Causes
1.
2.
3.
4.
5.

B. Effects
1.
2.
3.
4.
5.

I. ***Discrimination Because of Religion/Age/Sex***
  A. Causes
    1.
    2.
    3.
    4.
    5.
  B. Effects
    1.
    2.
    3.
    4.
    5.

I. ***Animals for Scientific Research***
  A. Causes
    1.
    2.
    3.
    4.
    5.
  B. Effects
    1.
    2.
    3.
    4.
    5.

Focus: *Cause and Effect—Practice in Organization*

Look at the lists you've brainstormed in the previous exercise and rearrange them in an *alternating chain* format: **AB AB AB AB AB.** Make sure to find the causes which directly relate to the effects.

Example:

I. ***High Divorce Rate in the United States***
  A. Cause
  B. Effect
  A. Cause
  B. Effect
  A. Cause
  B. Effect
  A. Cause
  B. Effect
  A. Cause
  B. Effect

I. ***The Cold War***
  A. Cause
  B. Effect
  A. Cause
  B. Effect
  A. Cause
  B. Effect
  A. Cause
  B. Effect
  A. Cause
  B. Effect

Exercise:

I. ***Increased Interest in Health-Related Hobbies***
  A.
  B.
  A.
  B.
  A.
  B.
  A.
  B.
  A.
  B.

I. ***Drug Abuse by Teenagers***
  A.
  B.
  A.
  B.
  A.
  B.
  A.
  B.
  A.
  B.

I. *The Women's Liberation Movement*
A.
B.
A.
B.
A.
B.
A.
B.
A.
B.

I. *The Popularity of ______ Music*
A.
B.
A.
B.
A.
B.
A.
B.
A.
B.

I. *High Suicide Rate Among Young People*
A.
B.
A.
B.
A.
B.
A.
B.
A.
B.

I. *The Increased Use of Computers*
A.
B.
A.
B.
A.
B.
A.
B.
A.
B.

I. *The Population Explosion*
A.
B.
A.
B.
A.
B.
A.
B.
A.
B.

I. *Starvation in Third World Countries*
A.
B.
A.
B.
A.
B.
A.
B.
A.
B.

I. *The Devaluation of ________ (Foreign Money)*
A.
B.
A.
B.
A.
B.
A.
B.
A.
B.

I. *Illegal Aliens*
A.
B.
A.
B.
A.
B.
A.
B.
A.
B.

I. ***The Generation Gap***
A.
B.
A.
B.
A.
B.
A.
B.
A.
B.

I. ***Violence on the Screen***
A.
B.
A.
B.
A.
B.
A.
B.
A.
B.

I. ***Discrimination Because of Age/Sex/Religion***
A.
B.
A.
B.
A.
B.
A.
B.
A.
B.

I. ***Animals for Scientific Research***
A.
B.
A.
B.
A.
B.
A.
B.
A.
B.

Focus:
Cause and Effect—Paragraph Practice

The following *connectors* will help you to tie your thoughts together in cause and effect paragraphs.

so, consequently, therefore, as a result, for this/these reasons, because of
in addition, besides, furthermore, another reason
first, second, third, finally

Exercise:

Now that you have completed the previous exercises on organization, try to write paragraphs based on the outlines you have written. Choose one which is in the *group approach* format with the **AAAAABBBBB** pattern and another in the *alternating chain approach* pattern **AB AB AB AB AB.** Use a separate sheet of paper.

CORRECTION

When you write, many ideas come to you at the same time. Part of the process of writing is to *revise* your ideas, *rearrange* your sentences, *change* words, and generally find the best way to put on paper the thoughts that are in your mind. This is not an easy job. It requires time and patience. In fact, it is almost impossible to create your best work after only one try.

An important part of the writing process is *revising*. You will find that your eraser is perhaps more important than your pen. Careful correction is part of the composition process.

In this section, some suggestions are given for *self-correction, peer correction,* and *teacher correction*. In addition, a progress report is included so that you can record the mistakes you make and watch how they disappear with practice.

Correction is not a final step. It is a constant part of the writing experience. Part of this process is to get suggestions from other people. Your teacher can help you and so can your classmates.

Focus:
Correction Symbols

These are the suggested symbols to be used for correction. Your teacher will review their meanings and examples with you in class.

Symbol	*Meaning*	*Example*	*Advice*
a	**Subject-Verb Agreement**	He *have*[a] a brother.	Verbs must agree with their subjects. What is the subject of this verb?
N	**Number Agreement**	They have two *pen*.[N]	Do you want to use the singular or plural form? Is it a *noncount* noun? How can you make a noncount noun *countable?*
Sp	**Spelling**	I *reede*[Sp] the newspaper.	Use your dictionary to find the correct spelling.
Pro	**Pronoun**	I like Mary. *He*[Pro] is my sister.	What (pro)noun does the pronoun refer to? Should it be singular or plural? Do you want an object pronoun or a subject pronoun?
Art	**Article**	[Art] *United States* is great! Can you give me *a*[Art] apple?	Is this the right article? Do you need *a, an,* or *the?* Is an article necessary? Did you forget an article?
Prep	**Preposition**	I live *in*[Prep] that street.	Is this the preposition you want? Is it necessary? Did you leave out a preposition?
WM	**Word Missing**	They ↑[WM] good students.	Did you forget a word—probably a subject or a verb?

Symbol	Meaning	Example	Explanation
WW	**Wrong Word or Phrase**	They *said* (WW) me the truth.	Find another way to say the same thing. You may need to rewrite only one word. Maybe you need to rewrite more than that.
WE	**Wrong Expression**	I am going to study *this* (WE) *night.* (WE)	Are you translating? This doesn't sound like English. Rewrite this and try to think in English.
WF	**Wrong Form**	You drive *careful.* (WF)	You need a different form of this word. Do you need a noun, a verb, an adjective, or an adverb?
WC	**Word Choice**	My neighbor is *stupid.* (WC)	This sounds mean or hard in English. Pay attention to your tone. Find a softer way to say the same thing.
↷	**Word Order**	We gave *to them the present.*	Is this English word order, or are you translating? Standard English word order is subject, verb, direct object, indirect object, adverbials of manner, place, and time.
( )	**Unnecessary**	I went shopping (*to*) downtown.	Remove this word or these words.
T	**Verb Tense**	I *study* (T) yesterday.	Did you use the right verb tense? Are there any time words to help you? What tense do you need? Present? Past? Future? Present Perfect?
VF	**Verb Form**	They *made* (VF) my watch in Japan.	What form of the verb should you use here? Passive? Active? Continuous? Infinitive? Past Participle? Gerund?

Symbol	*Meaning*	*Example*	*Advice*
?	**Unclear**	It has many ? *shrespgmldds.*	Something isn't clear. It may not make sense. It may have more than one meaning. It may be difficult to read. Rewrite it to make it clear.
P	**Punctuation**	Does he live in Vermont **P**	Do you need a question mark (**?**), a period (**.**), a comma (**,**), an exclamation point (**!**), or a semi-colon (**;**)? Is it time to begin a new sentence? Do you need a capital letter or an apostrophe (**'**) to show possession?
←©→	**Connect**	She is here. ←©→ Her government sent her.	Should these be separate sentences? What connector can tie these ideas together? Use a connector, a transition (bridge) word, or a time word to make this less choppy.
¶	**New Paragraph**	It is clear that he was a good child. ¶As an adult, he was always bad.	Do you have two very different thoughts in one paragraph? It is probably time to begin a new paragraph. Don't forget to indent.
r	**Repetition**	I live in Ann Arbor. **r** *Ann Arbor* is nice. **r** *Ann Arbor* is cold in the winter. **r** *Ann Arbor* has a university.	Have you said the same thing too many times? Can you say it another way by using pronouns? Rewrite and try not to repeat yourself.

Inc	**Incomplete Sentence (Fragment)**	Inc *Although she is my friend.*	Do you need a subject or a verb? Is this only a phrase or a clause, and not a complete idea?
//	**Parallel Structure**	We like reading and *to write.* //	Are your ideas balanced, or do you have a sentence which is made up of different word forms, i.e., gerunds, infinitives, adjectives, adverbs?
~~	**Run-on Sentence**	It was a nice day and the sun was shining and the birds were singing and we felt happy because it was Friday and there was no more school and we were going to a movie and after we wanted coffee.	This sentence is too long! You have many different sentences in one sentence. Break them apart. If this were spoken English, you would not have time to breathe. Let your hand rest. Use some punctuation.
R	**Rewrite**		Rewrite the composition or one section of the composition
1	**Not Again!**		You have made this error many times before. Find what you are doing wrong, and try to avoid the same mistake.
2	**Logic Problem**		This doesn't make sense. It doesn't follow what you have already said. It doesn't prove your point.
3	**Development**		You need to say more. You haven't given enough information.
4	**Lack of Unity**		Does this sentence belong in the paragraph? Is it covered by the topic sentence? If it doesn't *stick to* your topic, remove it.

Focus:
Progress Report

After you receive your graded compositions, you should chart your errors in order to see the progress you make. Fill in the number of mistakes of each type that you have made.

Composition Number

Kind of Error	1	2	3	4	5	6	7	8
Verb Tense (T)								
Spelling (Sp)								
Number Agreement (N)								
Subject-Verb Agreement (a)								
Word Missing (WM)								
Article (Art)								
Wrong Word (WW)								
Wrong Expression (WE)								
Wrong Form (WF)								
Punctuation (P)								
Preposition (Prep)								
Pronoun (Pro)								
Word Order (↜↝)								
Unnecessary ( )								
Verb Form (VF)								
Unclear (?)								
Connect (←©→)								
New Paragraph (¶)								
Repetition (r)								
Incomplete (Inc)								
Parallel Structure (//)								
Run-On Sentence (〰)								
Not Again! (1)								
Logic (2)								
Development (3)								
Lack of Unity (4)								

Focus: *Self-Correction—Check List*

Before you hand in your writing, check this list to be sure you have included the important rules you need to know.

1. Did you indent the first line of each paragraph, usually an inch (or 5 spaces)?
2. Have you written to the end of each line unless it is the end of the paragraph?
3. Is the left side of the paragraph even or straight in form? The right side should be even in form as much as possible. Is it?
4. Were you sure to write a title for each composition? This is *not* the topic. It is a title, like the title of a book. Was the title written with each word beginning with a capital letter, *except* for articles and prepositions?
5. Did you skip lines and skip pages? Have you written on every other line and every other page in order to allow enough room for your teachers or peers to make corrections and for you to be able to easily rewrite your composition?
6. Have you made sure your writing is *clear?* Can everyone read it?
7. Did you begin each sentence with a capital letter?
8. Did you end each sentence with a period (**.**), question mark (**?**), or exclamation mark (**!**)? Did you use commas (**,**) when you needed them?
9. Does each sentence have a subject and a verb?
10. Did you try not to use these words because they have lost their meaning through overuse?

nice	*stuff*	*something like that*
thing	*get*	*you know*

11. Have you avoided using more than one *and* in a sentence when possible?
12. Did you try to find and correct any errors in spelling, punctuation, agreement, or tense?

Focus: *Peer Group Correction—Organization*

Along with your teacher and classmates, read the following student composition. First, read it for *organization.* Answer the questions below by reading the student's work and discussing it with your teacher and peers.

Exercise:

<u>*A Important Person in my Live*</u>

Every people is important in live, but for me there is one person very special. and that one he is my father. My father is intelligent man because he know always what is the right thing. My mother very smart and she love him. Besides, my father is generous. He sends to me the money when I need them and he always gives advise to his friends and family. Furthermore, I respect my father because he is skillful. He can to fix the things when they broke. As I said you, my father important for me and for this I think in my openiun he special.

1. What is the *topic* or *umbrella* sentence?
2. What are the *specific points* of the body?
3. Do the specific points *stick to* the topic? In other words, are they included in the umbrella sentence?
4. Are the ideas tied together with *connectors?*
5. Is this boring to read? Is it *too* simple?
6. Is there something that could be better in this paragraph?
7. What *rhetorical device(s)* is/are used?

Focus:
Peer Group Correction—Grammar

You have worked with your classmates and teacher on correcting the organization of this paragraph. Now, work with those people to improve the *grammar.* After you reread the paragraph, ask yourself the questions below. Your teacher may want to vary this activity by directing your attention to one specific grammar point.

Exercise:

A Important Person in my Live

Every people is important in live, but for me there is one person very special. and that one he is my father. My father is intelligent man because he know always what is the right thing. My mother very smart and she love him. Besïdes, my father is generous. He sends to me the money when I need them and he always gives advise to his friends and family. Furthermore, I respect my father because he is skillful. He can to fix the things when they broke. As I said you, my father important for me and for this I think in my openiun he special.

1. Are words *spelled correctly?*
2. Do *subjects* and *verbs agree?*
3. Are the *verb tenses* correct?
4. Are *articles* used properly?
5. In general, does poor grammar stop you from understanding this paragraph?
6. Using *correction symbols,* can you suggest changes that make this a better composition? Make your changes directly on the paragraph.

Focus:
Paired Peer Correction

Your teacher will assign you a partner to work with. You and your partner will be given two other classmates' compositions to correct either individually, or together. Discuss the following questions about organization and content with your partner. Grammar is not important for this practice so don't correct it now.

Exercise:

Organization

1. Can you pull out a fast *outline* from this composition? ________________
2. Does it have a *topic* sentence? ________________
3. Do you like the *introduction?* Does it make you want to read more?

____

4. Is the *body* of the paragraph developed with *specific examples?* ________
5. Do the specifics come under the *umbrella* sentence? ________________
6. Do they come together with *connectors* and *transitions* or *bridge* sentences?

____

7. Is there a good *conclusion? Why do/don't you think so?* ________________

____

Content

1. Do you like this because it is *interesting?* ____________________
2. Does the writer use *good vocabulary?* ____________________
3. Are the *ideas* in the paragraph *developed* and *complete?* ____________
4. Does it sound like an *adult* wrote this paragraph? ______________
5. What do you want to say about this composition to make it better? ______

____

____

Focus: *Practice in Individual Correction of Specific Problems*

The following paragraphs written by students have some specific problems that are indicated in the directions. Use *correction symbols* to mark them.

Exercise:

1. In the following paragraph find four examples of *repetition* and use the correction symbol (**r**). Which connectors can you add to improve this? Comment on the *topic sentence.* What's wrong with the *specifics* in the outline? What other problems can you find?

Title: My Friend

I. My friend is a young man
   A. Businessman
   B. Good
   C. Careful

Conclusion: I am happy with my friend.

My Friend

My friend is a young man. He is a businessman at work. He is very nice man. He is a good English speaker. My friend is a good student. He is careful in the car. He is a careful man. I am happy with my friend.

2. In the following paragraph, find two errors in *verb tense* (**T**), two errors in *number agreement* (**N**) and two errors in *subject-verb agreement* (**a**).

Title: Taipei and Seattle

I. Taipei and Seattle have different things.
   A. Price
   B. Weather
   C. Streets

Conclusion: I lived in Seattle for a few days, so I like to compare them.

Taipei and Seattle

Taipei and Seattle have different things. Everythings are cheap in Taipei. In Seattle, everythings are more expensive. It is very warm in Seattle in summer. But Tapiei is hotter than Seattle, so people must with air conditioner. The streets look straight in Taipei. In Seattle there are less straight than Taipei beacuse Seattle is a small mountain. I live in Seattle a few days, so I like to compare them.

3. In the following paragraph, find five *preposition* (**Prep**) errors. Does the body go under the topic or umbrella sentence? What other problems can you find?

Title: My Father's Day

I. My father is busy in evry day so he always wakes up early in the morning.
   A. Morning
   B. Afternoon
   C. Evening

Conclusion: My father is very tired at night.

My Father's Day

My father is busy in evry day so he always wakes up early in the morning. He frequently wakes up early in the morning and usually drinks tow cups of coffee. He goes to work by car. At noon he comes back to home. He usually eats lunch late and he goes again to work by his car. At evening he usually comes back early and he is very tired because the work is very hard. He always eates dinner at 9:O'clock. My father is very tired at night.

4. Find four *article* (**Art**) errors in the following paragraph.

Title: A Dream I Remeber

I. Last Sunday I had a very bored dream when I watched the T.V.
   A. Showed
   B. Looked at the people
   C. Heard to the music

Conclusion: I was very a happy when I woke up from this dream because I was afraid.

A Dream I Remeber

Last Sunday I had a very bored dream when I watched the T.V. I looked at the T.V. and I saw the movie. I watched the Excorcist on channel 8 and I was afraid. I looked at the people; one of sombody climbed the wall and he jumped on man and he killed him. I saw man and he followed the boy and he killed him with the knife. I heard to the music and I shook my body. I saw some people and they didn't move on the floor and they fell on the floor. I was very afraid. I was very happy when I woke up from this dream because I was afraid.

5. Find three *spelling* (**Sp**) mistakes in this student's paragraph. Comment on the *introduction* and *conclusion*. What other problems can you find?

Title: My Future plans

I. I hope, I am not going to make mistakes in the future.
   A. Work
   B. Travel
   C. Interesting

Conclusion: I am going to learn every thing new and useful in the future.

My Future Plans

I hope, I am not going to make any mestaeks in the future. I will work in companie-oil. I am going to look for intrsting work. I will try to visit other countries on the holidays. I am going to learn many things from people. I will try to make my family happy. I am going to teach my children how to be happy in their life. I am going to learn everything new and useful in the future.

6. In the following student composition, the paragraph body isn't completely developed (**3**). What is missing? Improve this composition by adding to the *body* of the paragraph. What other problems can you find?

Title: The Problems of a Foreign Student in the United States

I. Students who study in foreign country have several problemes.

   A. Lonelyness

   B. Culture Shook

Conclusion: In conclusion. There are a couple problems foreign students have, such as lonliness and culture shook

The Problems of a Foreign Student in the United States

Students who study in foreign country have several problems. First of all, students feel lonly because they are away from their family. Lonelyness make them sad and depressed because Americans do not understand their language. Then, they might have culture shook because they have a different way to communicate with people and a different life style. In conclusion, foreign students might have some problems, such as lonelyness and culture shook. Some of American friend might help this foreign students.

3 The Product Through Process: Composing Paragraphs

Until now, you have had a lot of practice in the planning process. This led you to the development of paragraphs as a result of brainstorming and outlining. You have also practiced techniques for improving your writing which included rhetorical devices, connectors and correction strategies. You are now ready to practice writing paragraphs and applying all the information you have gotten so far. Your paragraphs should be *well-organized, grammatical* and *interesting*. You can make that happen by brainstorming and outlining.

In the next section, you will write paragraphs which include the entire process you have practiced. Models are provided as examples, but it is best to write on the required subjects from your own personal experiences. The paragraph models are organized according to grammatical and rhetorical target structures. A brief review of the grammar focus is presented before each paragraph. Your teacher will decide the areas in which you need practice and review the grammar and vocabulary points. You can go through the models together and notice how well they follow the outlines. Try to think about similar, though not identical, experiences to those presented.

Remember that a good paragraph begins with a general introductory or topic sentence. This is an umbrella for everything you say. It is the most important sentence because it catches the attention of your reader. The next part of the paragraph, the body, is specific and develops the main ideas presented in the topic sentence. The final part, the concluding sentence, ends the composition and makes it complete. Let your mind go. Brainstorm, organize, and write. Enjoy the process while you create a product—a composition.

GRAMMAR REVIEW: *SIMPLE PRESENT—THE VERB BE; THERE IS, THERE ARE*

Affirmative	*Negative*
I am = I'm a student. She is = She's a student. He is = He's a student. It is = It's a student. We are = We're students. You are = You're students. They are = They're students.	I am not = I'm not a student. She is not = She's not / She isn't a student. He is not = He's not / He isn't a student. It is not = It's not / It isn't a student. We are not = We're not / We aren't students. You are not = You're not / You aren't students. They are not = They're not / They aren't students.
Interrogative	***Also:*** There is = There's There are There is not = There's not. There isn't. There are not = There aren't. Is there? Yes, there is. No, there isn't. Are there? Yes, there are. No, there aren't.
(Why) Am I a student? Is she / he / it a student? Are we / you / they students?	

Spelling Rules	
Usually *add s* to 3rd person of *verbs.* *Examples:* He walks. She writes. It works.	*Add es* if the verb ends in *sh, ch, ss, x,* or *z.* *Examples:* She watches television. He washes the dishes. She misses her country. He fixes the car. He quizzes the class.
Change y to *i* and add *es* if a verb ends in a consonant + *y.* *Examples:* She studies.	*Add s* if a verb ends in a *vowel* + *y.* *Examples:* It pays. She plays. He stays.

Pronunciation Rules There are three different pronunciations for a simple present ending.		
[*s*](after a voiceless sound) walks works laughs	[*z*](after a voiced sound) loves listens gives	[*əs*] (after *s, sh, ch, x, z)* watches washes misses fixes quizzes

SIMPLE PRESENT IN CONTEXT

Example:

I am a foreign student. *She is* my classmate from China. *He is* her Indian friend. *It is* a nice group of classmates. *Everybody is* always here. *Nobody is* absent. *We are* happy in class because you are our teacher. *They are* French, Mexican, Japanese, and Arab. *There are* interesting people in our class.

Rhetorical Focus: *Description*

Grammar Focus: *Simple Present—The Verb BE; There Is, There Are*

Exercise:

On another sheet of paper, write about your family. You can talk about what each person does, or how many people there are, and what their names are. You only need to write eight sentences.

Example:

Title: My Family

Introduction: I. There are three other people in my family, and they are special to me.

A. Father

Body: B. Mother

C. Sister

Conclusion: I am lucky to have a close family.

My Family

There are three other people in my family, and they are very special to me. My father is a hard worker. He is a very nice man. In the same way, my mother is kind and beautiful. Her eyes are green, and her hair is black. My sister is a good artist. She is also my best friend. In conclusion, I am lucky to have such a close family.

Rhetorical Focus: ***Description Spatial Order***

Grammar Focus: ***Simple Present—The Verb BE; There Is, There Are***

Exercise:

Write a composition about your room using a separate sheet of paper. Use the verb *BE* in the *simple present tense.* Eight sentences will be enough at this time.

Example:

Title: My Classroom

Introduction: I. There are different things in my classroom.

A. Furniture

Body: B. Pictures

C. Windows

Conclusion: I am in class every day, thus, I like to look at the things in my classroom.

My Classroom

There are different things in my classroom. The furniture in this room is comfortable. The desks and chairs are near one another. In addition, there are many pictures on the wall. I like the map of the world because it is beautiful. What's more, the windows in my classroom are big and clean. There are pretty curtains on them. I am in class every day, thus, I like to look at the things in my classroom.

GRAMMAR REVIEW: *ADJECTIVES**

Affirmative	***Negative***
I am She, He, It is We, You, They are serious, glad, tired, sad, fast.	I am She, He, It is We, You, They are not serious.

Interrogative	
Am I Is she / he / it Are we / you / they serious?	What kind of person is she? He is a serious person. Which one is he? The serious one.

ADJECTIVES IN CONTEXT

I am a *good* daughter and sister.
She isn't *happy* because her grandmother is *sick*.
He is *tired* today. His eyes are *closed*.
It is a *small* car but it is *fast*. It isn't *noisy*.
We are *glad* to be in this *new* country.
You aren't *lonely* and *homesick* because you're a *friendly* person.
They are *intelligent* students. They are not *stupid*.

Questions: *What kind of* worker is he? He's a *hard* worker.
Which person is your friend? The *tall* one is my friend.

Rhetorical Focus: *Description*

Grammar Focus: *Adjectives*

Exercise:

On a separate sheet of paper, use adjectives to describe someone or something that you either love very much or that you really hate. Please try not to write more than eight sentences at this time.

Example:

Title: Lucas

Introduction: I. Lucas always makes me happy.

A. Friendly

Body: B. Cute

C. Loyal

Conclusion: Consequently, I love my dog very much.

See Appendix H for a list of adjectives in context.

Lucas

Lucas always makes me very happy. When I come home, he greets me at the door and jumps in the air. His long tail is always wagging back and forth when he sees me. I like to look at Lucas because he is adorable. For instance, he has a sweet face, big, sad eyes, and large feet. On top of that, my friend is faithful to me. He protects me in dangerous situations. Consequently, I love my dog very much.

Rhetorical Focus: *Description, Spatial Order*

Grammar Focus: *Prepositions and Adjectives*

Exercise:

Describe a place in your city or your country and use *prepositions*. Make sure to write eight sentences if possible. Please use a separate sheet of paper.

Example:

Title: My Street

Introduction: I. There are different things to see on my street.

A. Houses

Body: B. Trees

C. Cars

Conclusion: I think my street is a nice place to live.

My Street

There are different things to see on my street. Many lovely houses are next to each other where I live. Likewise, across the street from my house the houses are beautiful. There are some old trees around those houses. In autumn, the leaves fall to the ground below the trees. On my street, people always park their cars in front of their houses. One car is usually parked in back of another. I think my street is a nice place to live.

GRAMMAR REVIEW: *PRESENT CONTINUOUS*

Affirmative				*Negative*		
I	am	= I'm	running?	I am not	= I'm not	running.
She	is	= She's		She is not	= She's not She isn't	
He		= He's		He is not	= He's not He isn't	
It		= It's		It is not	= It's not It isn't	
We	are	= We're		We are not	= We're not We aren't	
You		= You're		You are not	= You're not You aren't	
They		= They're		They are not	= They're not They aren't	

Interrogative			**Also:**
(Where) Am	I	running?	There is = There's There are
Is	she he it		There is not = There's not There isn't There are not = There aren't
Are	we you they		Is there? Yes, there is. No, there isn't. Are there? Yes, there are. No, there aren't.

Spelling Rules					
Add -ing to most verbs.		*Drop* the *-e* before *-ing* if a verb ends in *-e*.		*Double the last consonant* before adding *-ing* if a verb ends in a *single vowel followed by a single consonant.*	
Examples:		*Examples:*		*Examples:*	
call	calling	come	coming	beg	begging
do	doing	give	giving	hit	hitting
find	finding	have	having	plan	planning
go	going	live	living	shop	shopping
read	reading	save	saving	trap	trapping

PRESENT CONTINUOUS IN CONTEXT*

I'*m sitting* in the movies now. Omar Sharif *is acting* in the movie. He'*s speaking* right now. An actress *is standing* next to Omar. She'*s looking* at him. Her new movie *isn't playing* today. It'*s opening* tomorrow.** We *are watching* the movie together. You *are enjoying* this movie, but those people *are talking,* and I can't hear Omar. They *are being* impolite.

**See Appendix G for a list of verbs that don't usually occur in the present continuous.*
***Note: The present continuous tense is sometimes used to express future.*

Rhetorical Focus: ***Description***

Grammar Focus: ***Present Continuous***

Exercise:

Look outside of your window and write about what you are looking at now. Make sure to use the *present continuous tense.* Write about eight sentences on a separate sheet of paper.

Example:

Title: Outside My Window

Introduction: I. Different things are happening outside my window.

A. Traffic

Body: B. Adults

C. Children

Conclusion: There is a world outside my window, and I am watching it.

Outside My Window

Different things are happening outside my window. First, many cars are passing in the street now. The police car is making a lot of noise. Second, older people are crossing the streets at the moment. One old man is walking and talking to his friend. Besides that, children are running on the sidewalk. At present, one boy is throwing a ball, and the other child is catching it. There is a world outside my window, and I am watching it.

Rhetorical Focus: ***Description***

Grammar Focus: ***Present Continuous***

Exercise:

Write a composition about what your mother, father, sister, brother, friend, aunt, uncle, or neighbor, is doing now. Make sure to use the *present continuous tense.* Please try not to write more than eight sentences, and use your own paper.

Example:

Title: My Niece

Introduction: I. I am watching my niece, and she is very busy now.

A. Playing

Body: B. Smiling

C. Talking

Conclusion: This baby is doing many things right now, and she is having fun.

My Niece

I am watching my niece, and she is very busy now. She is sitting on the floor with her toys. Her toy stuffed animal is lying next to her. My niece is smiling at the moment. She is laughing, and her little teeth are showing. She is showing something to me. My niece is making sounds and trying to talk. This baby is doing many things right now, and she is having fun.

GRAMMAR REVIEW: *POLITE COMMANDS; IMPERATIVES*

Polite Commands
Would you please pass the salt?
Could you give me the milk?
Please come to dinner.

Imperatives	
Go.	Don't go.
Turn.	Don't turn.
Walk.	Don't walk.

POLITE COMMANDS AND IMPERATIVES IN CONTEXT

Dear George,

Please *be* happy. *Find* another girlfriend. *Don't wait for* Martha to come back to you. *Forget* her! *Would you please call* me tonight? *Could you come* to my house for dinner? *Don't forget* to ask me to marry you! I will be a good first lady.

Love,
Abby

Rhetorical Focus: ***Chronological Order***

Grammar Focus: ***Polite Commands, Requests***

Exercise:

Imagine that you are in a position of authority like a parent, teacher, policeman, president, army sergeant, or employer and give somebody orders on *how* to do something. Use *polite commands* and/or *request forms* and write no more than eight sentences on a separate sheet of paper.

Example:

Title: The First Day at School

Introduction: I. It is important for you to learn some rules to follow on the first day of school.

A. Lateness

Body: B. Attendance

C. Studies

Conclusion: Please follow these regulations and you will do well.

The First Day at School

It is important for you to learn some rules to follow on the first day of school. For instance, do not be late to class. In other words, please try to come on time every day. Furthermore, be in class every day. Do not miss too many hours. Finally, study hard and do your homework carefully every night. Otherwise, you will not learn quickly. Please follow these regulations, and you will do well.

Rhetorical Focus:
Process, Spatial Order

Grammar Focus:
Polite Commands, Directions

Exercise:

Imagine that your friends call you from a nearby train or bus station in your home town, and they want to know how to get to your house. Politely give your friends directions to your house from the station. Try to use *request forms,* and please do not write more than eight sentences. Use your own paper.

Example:

Title:	Coming Home
Introduction:	I. When you follow these directions, it is easy to find my house.
	A. Train
Body:	B. Bus
	C. Walk
Conclusion:	Call me if you get lost!

Coming Home

When you follow these directions, it is easy to find my house. First, take the subway three stops and get out at West 4th Street. Next, cross the tracks and get on the next D train to Kings Highway, which is seven more stations. After that, go upstairs and head for the bus stop which is right outside the station. Then ride the No. 7 bus until Sheepshead Bay and get off there. Start to walk north for three blocks and turn left. Finally, continue left for one block until the traffic light, where you will see my house. Call me if you get lost!

GRAMMAR REVIEW: *ADVERBS OF FREQUENCY*

Affirmative	*Negative*
100% always **99–90%** usually **90–75%** often, frequently **75–25%** sometimes, occasionally	**0%** never **10–1%** rarely, hardly ever **25–10%** seldom, infrequently
Position	
1. They come *before* all verbs except the verb *BE*. They come *after BE*. Ex. She *always* arrives early. She is *always* early. 2. They come *between* an auxiliary and a main verb. Ex. She has *always* arrived on time.	

ADVERBS OF FREQUENCY IN CONTEXT

After the weekend, I'm *always* tired on Monday mornings. I am *never* ready for school.
Alberto *often* studies.
Mitsuko *rarely* studies. She doesn't like to study. She *usually* plays.
My friends and I *sometimes* go to a restaurant. We are *seldom* at home Saturday night.
Alberto and Mitsuko *hardly ever* come to the restaurant with us. They *occasionally* meet us at the movies after dinner.
What do you *usually* do on the weekends?

Rhetorical Focus: ***Description, Chronological Order***

Grammar Focus: ***Adverbs of Frequency—Simple Present***

Exercise:

Talk about your daily schedule or that of a close friend or relative. Make sure to use different *adverbs of frequency* (*usually, always, sometimes, never, seldom, rarely*) and try to limit yourself to about eight sentences. Use a separate sheet of paper.

Example:

Title: Elyse's Day

Introduction: I. My friend Elyse is a busy person; therefore, she always follows her daily schedule.

Body:
A. Morning
B. Afternoon
C. Evening

Conclusion: As a result of her long day, Elyse is always very tired at night.

Elyse's Day

My friend Elyse is a busy person; therefore, she always follows her daily schedule. An example of this is she frequently wakes up early in the morning and usually drinks a cup of coffee. Then she goes to work and often reads the newspaper on the way. At noon she rarely eats lunch. She sometimes walks outside for an hour; however, she seldom has time to relax because of her important job. My friend never walks home from work in the evening. On the contrary, she usually takes a taxi, although she occasionally rides the bus. As a result of her long day, Elyse is always very tired at night.

Rhetorical Focus: *Description*

Grammar Focus: *Adverbs of Frequency*

Exercise:

Write a composition about things you like or do not like to do. Make sure to use different *adverbs of frequency* (*usually, sometimes, never, always, often, rarely, seldom*). Please write no more than eight sentences, and use a separate sheet of paper.

Example:

Title: My Activities

Introduction: I. There are some things I like to do and other things I do not like to do.

Body:
A. Always
B. Sometimes
C. Never

Conclusion: People usually have different likes and dislikes.

My Activities

There are some things that I like to do and other things that I do not like to do. For instance, I always like to play with my dog at the park in the afternoon. We often go to different places and run together. In addition, I sometimes paint pictures at home in the evening. I occasionally play the guitar on the weekends with my friends. In contrast, since loud music hurts my ears, I seldom go to big concerts. It is never good for me to do things I don't like to do. People usually have different likes and dislikes.

GRAMMAR REVIEW: *SIMPLE PRESENT*

Affirmative		*Negative*						*Interrogative*		
I	work.	I	do not	work.	= I	don't	work.	(How) Do	I	work?
She He It	works.	She He It	does not		= She = He = It	doesn't		Does	she he it	
We You They	work.	We You They	do not		= We = You = They	don't		Do	we you they	

SIMPLE PRESENT TENSE IN CONTEXT

Every morning *I wake up* at 8:00.
My dog wakes me *up.*
My friend makes breakfast at 8:30.
She is a good cook, but *she doesn't like* to make coffee.
We usually *eat* breakfast together.
My friend and her brother go to school at 9:00 every day.
They come home at 6:00 every evening.
They don't have class at night.
When *do you get up* in the morning?
I have many friends from other countries.
María lives in Mexico.
She works every day.
Ahmed lives in France and *studies* engineering.
He's from Algeria.
We visit each other during vacations.
We often *write.*
You come from Japan.
I don't know how to speak Japanese.
My parents like my foreign friends. *They* always *invite* them to stay at our house because *foreigners don't have* friends and family in a new country.
They don't like to be alone.

Rhetorical Forms: *Description*

Grammar Focus: *Simple Present*

Exercise:

Write about your favorite hobby or thing to do when you have free time. You can also write about the hobbies of a classmate, friend, or relative. Use *simple present,* and please write about eight sentences on your own paper.

Example:

Title: Patty's Pastimes

Introduction: I. Patty spends a lot of her free time doing athletic activities. such as jogging, bicycling and swimming.

Body:
A. Jogging
B. Bicycling
C. Swimming

Conclusion: Patty is an active person; consequently, she enjoys sports in her free time.

Patty's Pastimes

Patty spends a lot of her free time doing athletic activities, such as jogging, bicycling and swimming. She likes to jog near her house. Similarly, she sometimes runs along the beach. What's more, Patty just got a new bicycle. She often rides it on the weekends with her friends. Besides that, Patty goes to the swimming pool every day after work. However, on sunny days, she prefers to swim outside. Patty is an active person; consequently, she enjoys sports in her free time.

Rhetorical Forms: *Description*

Grammar Focus: *Simple Present*

Exercise:

Write a composition about what you do every morning, afternoon, evening, weekend, etc. Make sure to use the *simple present tense.* Don't forget *s* in the third person—she, he, it. Write about eight sentences on a separate sheet of paper.

Example:

Title: Every Summer

Introduction: I. My family enjoys every summer in the country.

A. Swim

Body: B. Sail

C. Play

Conclusion: When we go to the country together, we always have a nice time.

Every Summer

My family enjoys every summer in the country. We have a house in the mountains on a lake. Where we swim, the water is usually cold and clear. We sometimes take our sailboat on the lake. The wind is strong so we move fast. On nice days, we play tennis outside. We often play volleyball with our friends. When we go to the country together, we always have a nice time.

GRAMMAR REVIEW: *COUNT AND NONCOUNT NOUNS*

	Count (How many?)	**Noncount Nouns (How much?)**
sg	*Examples:* a pen one pen	*Examples:* milk some milk a lot of milk lots of milk a little milk much milk
pl	*Examples:* pen*s* two pen*s* some pen*s* a lot of pen*s* a few pen*s* many pen*s*	

	Count (How many?)		**Noncount (How much?)**		
+	some +s	(pencil*s*)	some	(sugar_)	no *s*
−	any +s	(pencil*s*)	any	(sugar_)	no *s*
			much	(sugar_)	no *s*
?	any +s	(pencil*s*)	any	(sugar_)	no *s*

COUNT AND NONCOUNT NOUNS IN CONTEXT

Dear Mom,

I need *some advice.* My roommates and I want to have a *little party,* and I don't know what to do. We don't have *any problems* with space. We have *a lot of furniture* in our house. There are *many chairs, some tables,* and *a few sofas. A lot of people* can be comfortable. I need *some information* about food. There is *some fruit* in the refrigerator, but there aren't *any vegetables.* Also, we don't have *any dairy products.* I'm buying a *pound of cheese, some butter,* a *gallon of milk,* and a *loaf of French bread.* What about drinks? We have *some tea,* but we don't have *any coffee.* We also need *a little sugar.* We don't need *any* salt. People usually drink a *few cups* of coffee in the evening. I hope we have *lots of fun.* Mom, I hope you have a *little patience* with me. I don't have *much money.* Would you please lend me a *few dollars* to go shopping? Thanks *a lot.*

Love,
Natalie

Rhetorical Focus: ***Description, Classification***

Grammar Focus: ***Count and Noncount Nouns***

Exercise:

Describe a part of your country that you like and use *count* and *noncount* nouns. Discuss the geography of the place and try not to use more than eight sentences. Please write on a separate sheet of paper.

Example:

Title: New England

Introduction: I. The New England states have many beautiful qualities for all seasons.

A. Mountains and hills

Body: B. Lakes and oceans

C. Trees and flowers

Conclusion: It is always fun to visit the northeastern part of the United States.

New England

The New England states have many beautiful qualities for all seasons. For example, there are great numbers of mountains and hills, but no volcanoes. Lots of snow covers the mountains, and in winter people ski there, while in the summer there are many campers. In addition, many lakes are located in New England, and they are not terribly polluted. The Atlantic Ocean is along the coast, and there are a lot of fish and some other sea creatures. Besides water, there are numerous trees in this part of the United States, and some beautiful flowers. In fall, the trees have different colors, but in winter, there aren't any leaves on the branches and only a few flowers. It is always fun to visit the northeastern part of the United States.

Rhetorical Focus: ***Description, Classification, Chronological Order***

Grammar Focus: ***Count and Noncount Nouns***

Exercise:

Write a composition about what you usually buy in the store each week. Make sure to use *count* and *noncount* expressions. Try to write about eight sentences. Please use your own paper.

Example:

Title: The Supermarket

Introduction: I. Every week I buy many things at the store.

A. Dairy products

Body: B. Fruits and vegetables

C. Grains

Conclusion: I spend a lot of money when I buy food at the supermarket.

The Supermarket

Every week I buy many things at the store. I usually go to the dairy section first, and I buy a container of milk, a pound of butter, a dozen eggs, some cheese, and some yogurt. I never buy any margarine, but I sometimes buy a little cream. After that, I buy a head of lettuce, an ear of corn, a pound of mushrooms, some tomatoes, and a few onions. I also get a bag of apples, a bunch of bananas, and some oranges in the fruit section. My last stop is the grain department where I pick up a box of cereal, a loaf of bread, and a few other things. I don't buy any beans, but I often get a little rice. I spend a lot of money when I buy food at the supermarket.

GRAMMAR REVIEW: *SIMPLE PAST—THE VERB BE; DEMONSTRATIVE ADJECTIVES AND IRREGULAR PLURALS*

Affirmative	*Negative*	*Interrogative*
I / She / He / It } was sad.	I / She / He / It } was not } wasn't sad.	(Where) Was { I? / she? / he? / it?
We / You / They } were sad.	We / You / They } were not } weren't sad.	Were { we? / you? / they?

GRAMMAR REVIEW: *DEMONSTRATIVE ADJECTIVES AND IRREGULAR PLURALS*

Singular	*Plural*
This man (here)	These men (here)
That man (there)	Those men (there)

Examples:

This/That woman	These/Those women
This/That child	These/Those children
This/That tooth	These/Those teeth
This/That person	These/Those people
This/That foot	These/Those feet
This/That mouse	These/Those mice
This/That fish	These/Those fish
This/That sheep	These/Those sheep

SIMPLE PAST OF BE, DEMONSTRATIVE ADJECTIVES AND IRREGULAR PLURALS IN CONTEXT

This car next to me was expensive.
That car over there was cheap.
These children were in my class.
Those people across the street were not my students.
This woman near me was my teacher.
That man near you wasn't at the party.
Who were *those* men and women on the television?

Rhetorical Focus: *Description*

Grammar Focus: *There is, There are, Past of BE*

Exercise:

Describe the best present you have ever received. Make sure to write in the *past tense* and to use the verb *BE*. Write no more than eight sentences if possible, and use your own paper.

Example:

Title: My Favorite Present

Introduction: I. When I received my favorite present, it was a very special moment for me.

Body:
A. Size
B. Color
C. Feeling

Conclusion: My favorite present was, and still is, my dog Lucas.

My Favorite Present

When I received my favorite present, it was a very special moment for me. My friend brought him, and he was very small and round. The puppy was able to fit under the bed, in the drawers, or in my pockets. This nice dog was almost completely black. However, there were a few white spots on his face, chest, and feet. He was very smooth and soft. Besides that, he was always warm. My favorite present was, and still is, my dog Lucas.

Rhetorical Focus: ***Description***

Grammar Focus: ***Past of BE, Demonstrative Adjectives***

Exercise:

Talk about some things you bought in a store. Discuss the things you saw with *demonstrative adjectives* (*this, that, these, those*) and the verb *BE* in the *past tense*. Write about eight sentences if possible on your own paper.

Example:

Title: My Purchases

Introduction: I. There were beautiful things to buy in the department store yesterday.

A. Blouse and pants

Body: B. Coat, hat, and gloves

C. Shoes and boots

Conclusion: All of these clothes were not expensive because they were on sale at the store yesterday.

My Purchases

There were a lot of beautiful things to buy in the department store yesterday. For example, this pretty shirt was a good deal. Also, those pants were on special yesterday, so they were cheap. This coat and that hat were on the second floor of the store. These gloves were a bargain too. Those shoes were the wrong size, but they were the last pair. These vinyl boots were very comfortable. All of these clothes were not expensive because they were on sale at the store yesterday.

GRAMMAR REVIEW: *SIMPLE PAST*

Affirmative	*Negative*	*Interrogative*
I / She / He / It / We / You / They } talked / played / lasted } for a long time.	I / She / He / It / We / You / They } did not talk. / didn't	(When) Did { I / she / he / it / we / you / they } talk?

Spelling Rules		
Add d to verbs that end in *e*. *Examples:* bake—baked chase—chased die—died dance—danced love—loved	*Add -ed* if a verb does not end in *e*. *Examples:* ask—asked call—called dream—dreamed talk—talked	*Double the last consonant* and *add -ed* if a one-syllable verb ends with a *single vowel followed by a single consonant.* *Examples:* beg—begged pin—pinned pit—pitted shop—shopped trap—trapped
Change y to *i* and add *-ed* if a verb ends in a *consonant* + *y*. *Examples:* cry—cried study—studied worry—worried	*Do not change y* to *i* and add *-ed* if the verb ends in a *vowel* + *y*. *Examples:* enjoy—enjoyed stay—stayed	

Pronunciation Rules		
[*t*] (after a voiceless sound) *Examples:* walked worked laughed	[*d*] (after a voiced sound) *Examples:* loved listened	[ə*d*] (after *t* or *d*) *Examples:* wanted needed

SIMPLE PAST IN CONTEXT

Last weekend *I tried* to do different things with friends and family. For instance, *I studied* on Friday. That night, my *father asked* me some questions about school. Then, my *mother talked* to my father. *We didn't stay* together on Saturday night. My *parents watched* television, but your *parents didn't. They visited* their friends. *You called* me the day before yesterday. *You enjoyed* your weekend, and *I did* too.

Rhetorical Focus: ***Narration***

Grammar Focus: ***Simple Past***

Exercise:

Remember something in the past that you experienced for the first time. This might be a trip, a new food, a date, or anything that was new to you at the time. Limit yourself to the *past tense* and to about eight sentences if you can. Use your own paper.

Example:

Title: When I Left Home

Introduction: I. The first time that I did not live with my family, I was very homesick.

A. Visit

Body: B. Talk

C. Call

Conclusion: I wanted to see my family very soon after I left home.

When I Left Home

The first time that I did not live with my family, I was very homesick. My friend from home lived near me, and I visited her every day. We stayed together all the time and remembered nice things about home. During those moments, we often talked about our friends and family. We discussed our feelings with each other. After that, we used to call our families. I used the telephone very often at that time. I wanted to see my family very soon after I left home.

Rhetorical Focus:
Narration, Spatial Order

Grammar Focus:
Simple Past and Prepositions

Exercise:

Write a composition about a time you lost something and where you looked for it. Make sure to use *prepositions*. Write about eight sentences if possible, and use a separate sheet of paper.

Example:

Title: The Missing Keys

Introduction: I. Yesterday my friend lost her keys, and she looked for them all over her house.

Body:
A. Kitchen
B. Living room
C. Bedroom

Conclusion: At night, my friend laughed because she found them in her pocket.

The Missing Keys

Yesterday my friend lost her keys, and she looked for them all over the house. At first, she checked under the table, on the chairs, and in the refrigerator in the kitchen. After that, she tried to find them behind the stove. In the living room, she moved the sofa and searched below it. She did not see them between the chairs either. In the bedroom, they were not beside her bed. She could not find them on top of her dresser or in her drawers. At night, my friend laughed because she found them in her pocket.

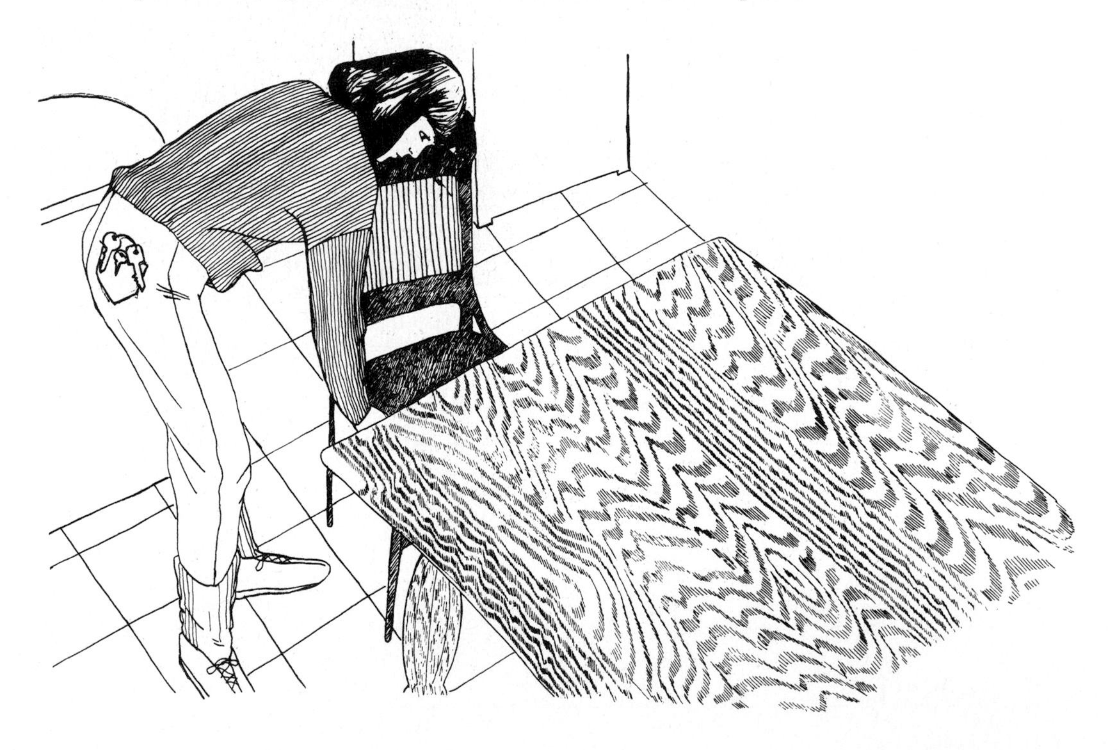

GRAMMAR REVIEW: *IRREGULAR PAST**

Affirmative		*Negative*			*Interrogative*		
I		I				I	
She		She		run.		she	
He	ran.	He	did not	go.		he	run?
It	went.	It	didn't	eat.	(How often) Did	it	go?
We	ate.	We		fly.		we	eat?
You	flew.	You				you	fly?
They		They				they	

IRREGULAR PAST IN CONTEXT

A Bad Day

I *had* a bad day yesterday. Everything *went* wrong. First, my alarm clock *didn't ring*. Because of that, I *woke up* late. I *didn't go* to my first class, so I *was* marked absent. Moreover, I *caught* a cold the same day. I *drank* orange juice and *took* Vitamin C. Then, I *made* breakfast. I *ate* one piece of toast before the toaster *broke*. After that I *went* to school. I *drove* but I *didn't have* any gas. I *forgot*** *to put* gas in the car, and I *left* my wallet at home. Also, I *didn't bring* my keys. At school, I *sat* in the last row. The teacher *spoke* to me, but I *didn't say* anything because I *didn't know* the correct answer. As a result, I *got* a bad grade. The teacher *told* me to go home. When I *got* home, I *thought* about my day and *felt* bad. I *slept* for a long time. My roommates *found* me on the sofa. What a day!

Rhetorical Focus: ***Narration***

Grammar Focus: ***Simple Past—Irregular and Regular Forms***

Exercise:

Write about your first day in the United States. Make sure to use the *past* tense. Please try to write about eight sentences, and use your own paper.

Example:

Title: My First Day in France

Introduction: I. I felt very surprised my first day in France.

A. Language

Body: B. Prices

C. Food

Conclusion: To conclude, the first time doing anything is always a little difficult.

My First Day in France

I felt very surprised my first day in France. I didn't know the language very well; as a result, I couldn't understand the people. Everyone spoke very fast, and I read the signs wrong. Furthermore, the prices were high in Paris, and I paid a lot of money for the taxi. I also forgot to change money at the airport, so I needed to pay more money at the bank. I was hungry later,

*See Appendix K for a complete list.

***The past perfect tense, had + past participle,* is often used with two or more actions in the past. The past perfect indicates the *earlier* of the two actions. (*Example:* I didn't have any gas because I *had forgotten* to fill the tank earlier.) However, for the purpose of simplification, past perfect is not used in this text.

and the food looked good, but I didn't know what to eat. I ordered an omelette because I knew the name. To conclude, the first time doing anything is always a little difficult.

Rhetorical Focus: ***Narration***

Grammar Focus: ***Simple Past—Irregular and Regular Forms; Adjectives***

Exercise:

Write a composition about a dream you had in the past. Try to describe the dream with *adjectives* and make sure to use the *past tense.* Write about eight sentences on a separate sheet of paper.

Example:

Title: A Dream I Remember

Introduction: I. Last night I had an interesting dream.

A. Colors

Body: B. People

C. Music

Conclusion: I felt sorry when I woke up from that dream.

A Dream I Remember

Last night I had an interesting dream. There were many different colors, and everything looked beautiful. For instance, the sky was clear blue, and the grass was bright green. I saw and knew many people from my childhood in that dream. We walked together and talked as we remembered our pasts. I heard loud music, and I didn't see where the music came from. I finally found a piano player near a rainbow. I felt sorry when I woke up from that dream.

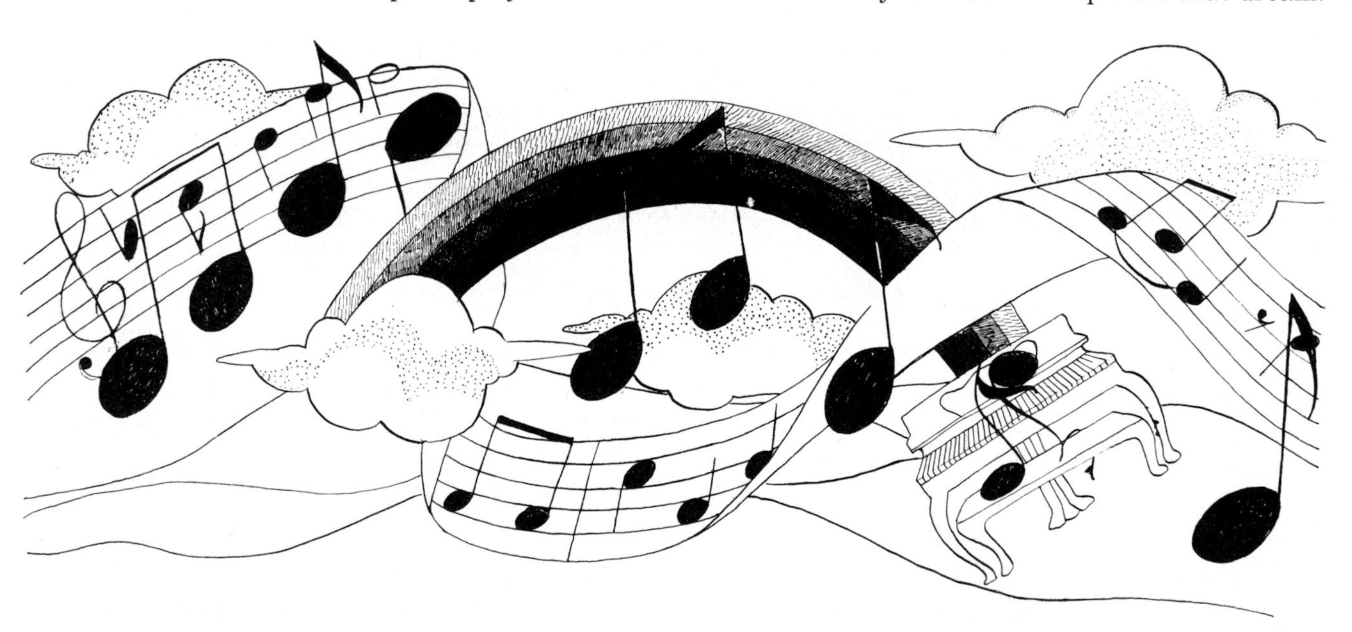

GRAMMAR REVIEW: MODALS*—CAN = AM / IS / ARE ABLE TO

Affirmative	*Negative*	*Interrogative*
I She He It We You They can work.	I She He It We You They cannot work. can't	(How) Can I she he it we you they work?

GRAMMAR REVIEW: MODALS—COULD = WAS / WERE ABLE TO

Affirmative	*Negative*	*Interrogative*
I She He It We You They could work.	I She He It We You They could not work. couldn't	(How) Could I she he it we you they work?

MODALS IN CONTEXT

I can speak Spanish and French. *I couldn't* when I was a child.
You can't speak Spanish, but *you can speak* French. *Could you* last year?
Is your sister able to speak another language? *Can she speak* Italian?
Your brother *can swim* well. *Can you run* fast? *Were you* always *able to run* fast?
We can't be late for class but *we can be* early.
They can't give us a ride to school. *We can take* the bus.

Rhetorical Focus: *Comparison and Contrast*

Grammar Focus: *Modals—Can, Could*

Exercise:

Remember the things you *could* do as a child but *cannot* do as an adult. Otherwise you can write about the things you *could not* do as a child but *are able* to now. Limit yourself to about eight sentences and use the modals *can* and *could.* Please use a separate sheet of paper.

Example:

Title: Then and Now

Introduction: I. When I was younger, I was able to do many things I cannot do now.

A. Carefree

Body: B. Inexpensive

C. Uninhibited

Conclusion: Life was fun and easy when I was a child.

See Appendix I for a review of Modals.

Then and Now

When I was younger, I was able to do many things that I cannot do now. One example of this is that my parents could make my decisions for me when I was a child; consequently, I never had to worry. In contrast, now I cannot burden my mother and father with all of my responsibilities. As a child, I could ride public transportation for free by sitting on my parents' knees. However, as an adult I cannot go many places without paying. In my youth, I could learn languages, sports, and instruments more easily. On the other hand, as I get older, I cannot do things as freely because I am more inhibited. Life was fun and easy when I was a child.

Rhetorical Focus: ***Description, Classification***

Grammar Focus: ***Modals—Can, Could***

Exercise:

Discuss the abilities of a person whom you admire and hope to be like. Make sure to use the modals *can* and *could.* Please write no more than eight sentences if possible. Use another sheet of paper.

Example:

Title: My Grandmother

Introduction: I. Grandma is able to do many kinds of things.

Body:
- A. Can cook and bake
- B. Can sew and knit
- C. Can play music and sing

Conclusion: People who can do different things well are very lucky and talented.

My Grandmother

Grandma is able to do many kinds of things. For example, she can cook food that always tastes wonderful. She is also able to bake delicious cakes, cookies, and cupcakes. Furthermore, my grandmother could always make beautiful clothes because she can sew very well. Besides that, she knits lovely, warm sweaters. Moreover, this special woman can play balalaika and piano beautifully. She was always able to sing sweetly, and she still can. People who can do different things well are very lucky and talented.

GRAMMAR REVIEW: *FUTURE*

WILL

Affirmative		*Negative*		*Interrogative*
I will play.	= I'll	I will not play.	= I won't play.	(What) Will I play?
She will play.	= She'll	She will not play.	= She won't play.	(What) Will she play?
He will play.	= He'll	He will not play.	= He won't play.	(What) Will he play?
It will play.	= It'll	It will not play.	= It won't play.	(What) Will it play?
We will play.	= We'll	We will not play.	= We won't play.	(What) Will we play?
You will play.	= You'll	You will not play.	= You won't play.	(What) Will you play?
They will play.	= They'll	They will not play.	= They won't play.	(What) Will they play?

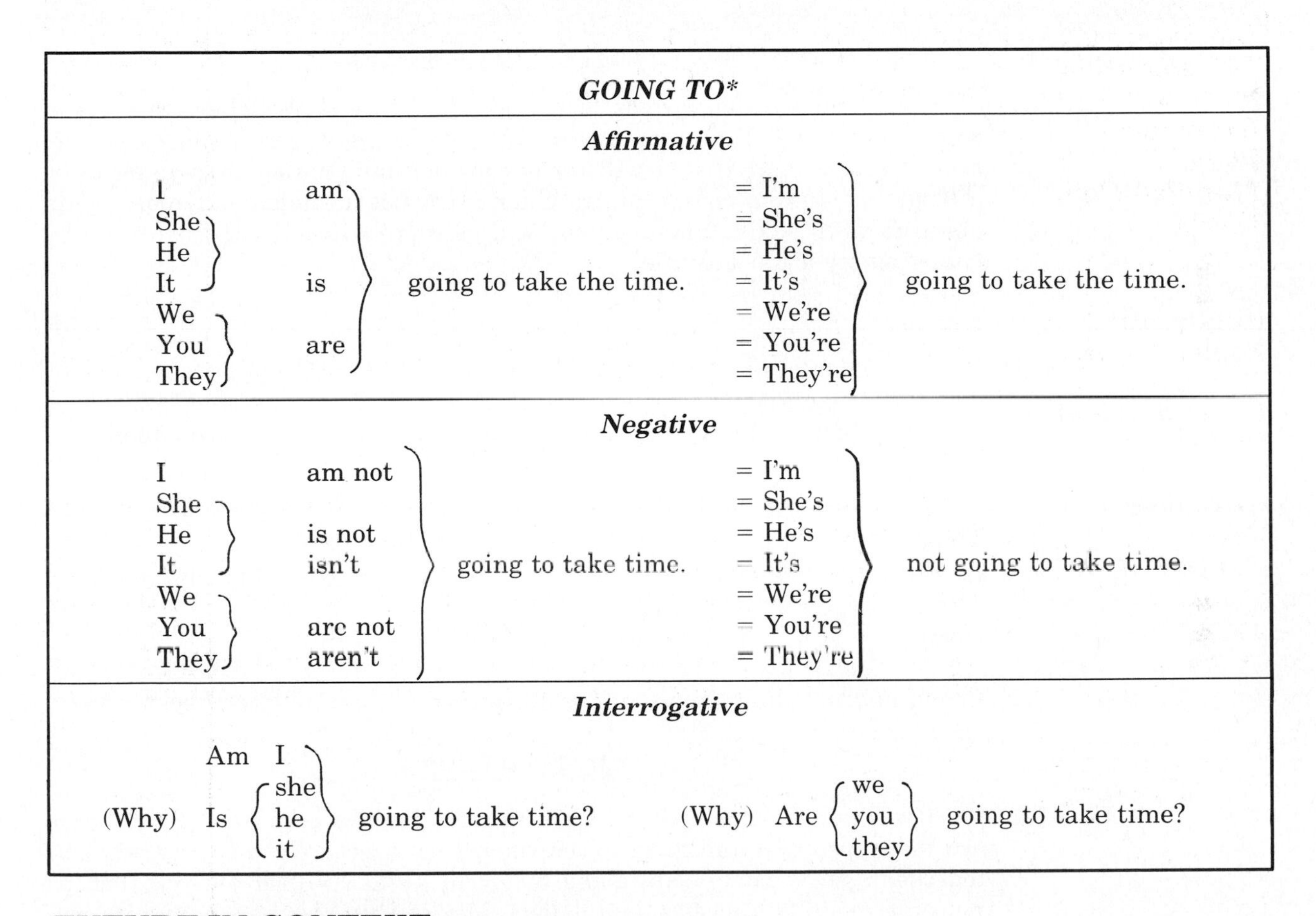

GOING TO*

Affirmative

I	am going to take the time.	= I'm	going to take the time.
She	is going to take the time.	= She's	going to take the time.
He	is going to take the time.	= He's	going to take the time.
It	is going to take the time.	= It's	going to take the time.
We	are going to take the time.	= We're	going to take the time.
You	are going to take the time.	= You're	going to take the time.
They	are going to take the time.	= They're	going to take the time.

Negative

I	am not going to take time.	= I'm	not going to take time.
She	is not / isn't going to take time.	= She's	not going to take time.
He	is not / isn't going to take time.	= He's	not going to take time.
It	is not / isn't going to take time.	= It's	not going to take time.
We	are not / aren't going to take time.	= We're	not going to take time.
You	are not / aren't going to take time.	= You're	not going to take time.
They	are not / aren't going to take time.	= They're	not going to take time.

Interrogative

Am I going to take time?	(Why) Are we going to take time?
(Why) Is she going to take time?	(Why) Are you going to take time?
(Why) Is he going to take time?	(Why) Are they going to take time?
(Why) Is it going to take time?	

FUTURE IN CONTEXT

I won't be rich when I finish school. *I will be* educated, but *I won't take* any trips. Some *students won't have* enough money to travel. *They aren't going to visit* other countries next year. However, *Tobias is going to travel* next summer. *Mary will go* with him. *Tobias and Mary will have* a great trip. *They are going to send* us postcards.

*Note: *Going to* is often pronounced *gonna* in spoken English but should not be written this way.

Rhetorical Forms: ***Narration, Chronological Order***

Grammar Focus: ***Future***

Exercise:

Write a composition about what you will do after you finish your studies. Make sure to use both *future tenses—will, BE + going to,* and please try not to write more than eight sentences. Use a separate sheet of paper.

Example:

Title: My Future Plans

Introduction: I. I am going to do various things in the future.

A. Travel

Body: B. Study

C. Work

Conclusion: I will learn a lot by changing my usual activities.

My Future Plans

I am going to do various things in my future. First, there are lots of countries I will visit in a few years. I am going to see different places, people, and customs. After that, I will try to continue my studies. It is going to be difficult to study after traveling. When I am not a student anymore, I am going to work again. I hope my job will be interesting. I will learn a lot by changing my usual activities.

Rhetorical Focus: ***Narration, Chronological Order***

Grammar Focus: ***Future***

Exercise:

Write a composition about what you are going to do when you return to your country. Make sure to use both forms of the future tenses—*will* and *BE + going to.* Write just eight sentences if possible, and use your own paper.

Example:

Title: My Future Trip

Introduction: I. I will be very busy when I visit Mexico City the next time.

A. People

Body: B. Places

C. Things

Conclusion: I am going to take advantage of the time that I spend there.

My Future Trip

I will be very busy when I visit Mexico City the next time. First, there are many people I am going to see when I get there. We will be glad to be together again. Next, I am going to try to go to cultural events, such as museum exhibits, concerts, and ballets. Mexico City also has many interesting restaurants where I will eat. Finally, there will be a lot of different things to buy there. I hope clothes and crafts will be on sale when I go to the market. I am going to take advantage of the time that I spend there.

GRAMMAR REVIEW: *POSSESSIVES*

Subject Pronouns	*Possessive Adjectives*	*Possessive Pronouns*
I	My	Mine
She	Her	Hers
He	His	His
It	Its	—
We	Our	Ours
You	Your	Yours
They	Their	Theirs

POSSESSIVES IN CONTEXT

This is *my* book. It's not *yours*.
That book is *yours*. It isn't *mine*.
Her notebook is on the desk. It is *hers*.
His papers are not on *his* desk. They are on *her* desk, but they are *his*.
Our classroom is bigger than yours. *Ours* is the blue room.
Yours is smaller than *ours*. *Your* room is green.
Their room isn't comfortable. *Theirs* is always cold.

Rhetorical Focus: ***Narration, Description***

Grammar Focus: ***Possessives***

Exercise:

Write about your favorite possession or about the favorite possession of your friend, sister, brother, mother, father, teacher, or classmate. Use *possessive adjectives,* and write no more than eight sentences if possible. Use a separate sheet of paper.

Example:

Title: Possessions

Introduction: I. Many people have possessions that they love.

A. Mother's

Body: B. Father's

C. Sister's

Conclusion: People often become sentimental about the things they own.

Possessions

Many people have possessions that they love. For instance, my mother's family pictures are her favorite. She and my father enjoy looking at their children's photographs. My father's favorite thing that he owns is our house. He loves to work with his tools and to relax there. Another example of a favorite possession is my sister's art supplies. She uses them to create her most beautiful pictures. People often become sentimental about the things they own.

Rhetorical Focus: *Narration, Description*

Grammar Focus: *Possessives*

Exercise:

Discuss a day when you were in a group, and you had to identify things that belonged to you and to different people. This experience could have been in camp, at a store, at a bazaar, at a lost and found, or anything which might involve people's property. Be sure to use *possessive forms* and try to write eight sentences if possible. Please use your own paper.

Example:

Title: The Garage Sale

Introduction: I. Many of us bought things at the garage sale that we had to identify at the end of the day.

A. Mine and ours

Body: B. Theirs

C. His and hers

Conclusion: All of us were quite satisfied with our new purchases.

The Garage Sale

Many of us bought things at the garage sale that we had to identify at the end of the day. My antique dresser was beautiful, and the desk lamp at the right was mine too. Our family got some pretty wall hangings, and the brass bed was also ours. My friends' property was in the corner of the garage. In fact, the old photograph next to the sofa was theirs. A young girl wanted some old books behind the table, and the owner told her that the books belonged to him. Her brother bought the table because it was like his old table. All of us were quite satisfied with our new purchases.

GRAMMAR REVIEW: *PAST CONTINUOUS*

Affirmative			*Negative*			*Interrogative*		
I She He It	was	working.	I She He It	was not wasn't	working.	(When) Was	I she he it	working?
We You They	were		We You They	were not weren't		Were	we you they	

PAST CONTINUOUS IN CONTEXT

The Substitute Teacher

The English teacher was absent yesterday. The students *were doing* many things when the new teacher arrived. I *was looking* out the window. You *were talking*. Yoshi *was laughing* when she opened the door. Mehdi *was writing* on the blackboard. We *weren't listening* to the new teacher. The other students *were jumping* up and down. When the substitute teacher went home, she *was feeling* angry.

Rhetorical Focus: *Narration, Chronological Order*

Grammar Focus: *Past Continuous*

Exercise:

Write about something you were going to do, or intended to do, but never did. You can use an example from yesterday, last night, last year, or years ago. Use the *past continuous tense* and write about eight sentences on your own paper.

Example:

Title: Good Intentions

Introduction: I. Last week, though I had a lot of ideas about what I was going to do on the weekend, I never accomplished my goals.

Body:
A. Write some letters
B. Clean the house
C. Finish my book

Conclusion: Although my intentions were good, I did not do anything I was going to do.

Good Intentions

Last week, though I had a lot of ideas about what I was going to do on the weekend, I never accomplished my goals. All week, I thought that I was going to write letters on the weekend. While I was answering my first letter, my friend called me, so I could not finish it. In addition, my roommates and I were planning to clean the house. Yet, when the time came to begin, everyone was doing something else. Later, I was planning to finish my book. While I was reading, I fell asleep. Although my intentions were good, I did not do anything I was going to do.

Rhetorical Focus:
Narration

Grammar Focus:
Past Continuous and Simple Past

Exercise:

Recall an interesting, strange, embarrassing, funny, or frightening experience that happened to you *while you were doing something else*. Make sure to show the contrast between the *past continuous* and *simple past tenses*. Limit yourself to about eight sentences. Please use your own paper.

Example:

Title: An Unforgettable Trip

Introduction: I. Some interesting things happened to us on our way to Granada, Spain.

A. Bus driver

Body: B. Bus passengers

C. Bus ride

Conclusion: When we finally got to Granada, we realized that strange things happen when we don't expect them to.

An Unforgettable Trip

Some interesting things happened to us on our way to Granada, Spain. While we were waiting to buy train tickets in Barcelona, a bus driver came over to my friend and me. He told us he was going to go to Granada and that the ride was cheap, and the bus was air-conditioned. When we met some other people at the station, they said they were traveling on the same bus. While we were getting on the bus, the Spanish passengers told us not to worry. However, the bus was making a lot of noise, and while we were moving fast, smoke was passing through the bus. When the bus stopped, all of us were trying to have a good time dancing, singing, and laughing, but we were a little afraid. When we finally got to Granada, we realized that strange things happen when we don't expect them to.

GRAMMAR REVIEW: *VERBS AND ADJECTIVES*

Perception Verbs + Adjectives	
Examples:	
feel	become
smell	be (am, is, are, was, were, will be)
taste	
sound	
look	
appear	
seem	

VERBS AND ADJECTIVES IN CONTEXT

1. **Feel** Puppies feel *soft.*
   The athletes felt *healthy.*
2. **Smell** The garbage smelled *awful.*
   Her cake smelled *delicious.*
3. **Taste** The Indian food will taste *spicy.*
   The lemon tasted *sour.*
4. **Sound** The rock band sounded *good.*
   She sounds (seems) *happy.*
5. **Look** The car looked *old.*
6. **Appear** The couple appeared *happy.*
7. **Seem** The workers seemed *tired.*
8. **Become** He will become *bald* in his thirties.
   They are going to become more *relaxed* after the test.
9. **Be:**

am	I *am* not old.	**was**	She *was* busy.
is	It *is* foggy today.	**were**	The men *were* very careful.
are	Cats *are* not dirty animals.	**will be**	I *will be* late.

Rhetorical Focus: ***Narration, Description, Classification***

Grammar Focus: ***Verbs and Adjectives***

Exercise:

Write about a big meal that you had on some special occasion in your country. Describe the food with all your senses. Remember that *sense (perception) verbs* are followed by *adjectives.* Also, make sure to write about eight sentences. Use a separate sheet of paper.

Example:

Title: A Vegetarian Thanksgiving

Introduction: I. I felt very happy once my friends decided to prepare a vegetarian Thanksgiving dinner.

Body:
A. Look
B. Smell
C. Taste

Conclusion: The idea of a vegetarian Thanksgiving sounds strange; nevertheless, it was wonderful.

A Vegetarian Thanksgiving

I felt very happy once my friends decided to prepare a vegetarian Thanksgiving dinner. At first, all the food looked tempting. The different dishes, such as vegetables, fruit and cheeses, seemed very fresh and tasty. What is more, the room smelled warm and appeared cozy. Moreover, the fragrance of pies, casseroles, quiches and breads filled the air. Of course, the food tasted delicious! All the guests tried a little of everything. The idea of a vegetarian Thanksgiving may sound strange; nevertheless, it was wonderful.

Rhetorical Focus: ***Description, Classification***

Grammar Focus: ***Verbs and Adjectives***

Exercise:

Imagine that you are trying to describe your country to a person who has never been there. Use all of your *senses*—sight, smell, taste, touch, and hearing, and try to write the description in eight sentences. Please use your own paper.

Example:

Title: My Home Town

Introduction: I. New York City has many qualities to remember.

A. Looks

Body: B. Sounds, smells, and tastes

C. Feelings

Conclusion: I use all of my senses when I think about New York.

My Home Town

New York City has many qualities to remember. For instance, the buildings look very tall and narrow in Manhattan. Sometimes the sky seems gray and other times it appears clear. Furthermore, in the streets of New York the cars sound noisy, but the musician's music sounds beautiful. Not only that, the food in the different restaurants smells delightful and everything tastes delicious. People are interested in New York because it is an exciting city. It feels wonderful to visit there. I use all my senses when I think about New York.

GRAMMAR REVIEW: *ADJECTIVES* AND ADVERBS*

1. Adjectives that end in *y: Change* the *y* to *i* and *add -ly* to form the adverb. *Examples:* happy → happily busy → busily
2. (a) Adjectives that end in *e: Add -ly* to form the adverb. (The *e* usually remains.) *Examples:* sincere → sincerely active → actively
(b) Adjectives that end in *le: Change* the final *e* to *y* to form the adverb. (No *e*) *Examples:* probable → probably possible → possibly
3. Adjectives that end in *l: Add -ly* to form the adverb. (There will be a double *l*.) *Examples:* professional → professionally careful → carefully
4. Adjectives that end in *ic: Add -ally* to form the adverb. *Examples:* fantastic → fantastically enthusiastic → enthusiastically
5. All other adjectives: *Add -ly* to form the adverb.
6. Be careful when you change these adjectives to adverbs. They are *irregular*. *Examples:* good → well   straight → straight fast → fast   early → early hard → hard   late → late loud → loud

*See Appendix H for complete list of adjectives.

ADJECTIVES AND ADVERBS IN CONTEXT

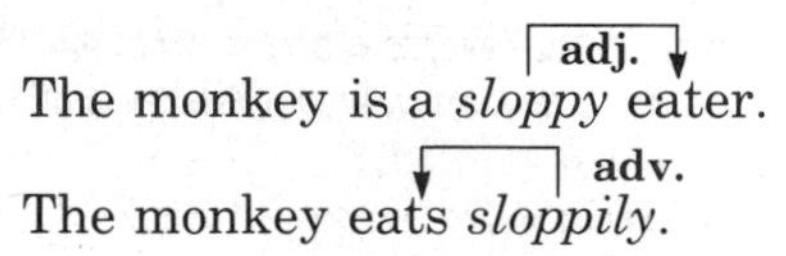

adj.
The monkey is a *sloppy* eater.
adv.
The monkey eats *sloppily*.

adj.
The birds are *beautiful* singers.
adv.
The birds sing *beautifully*.

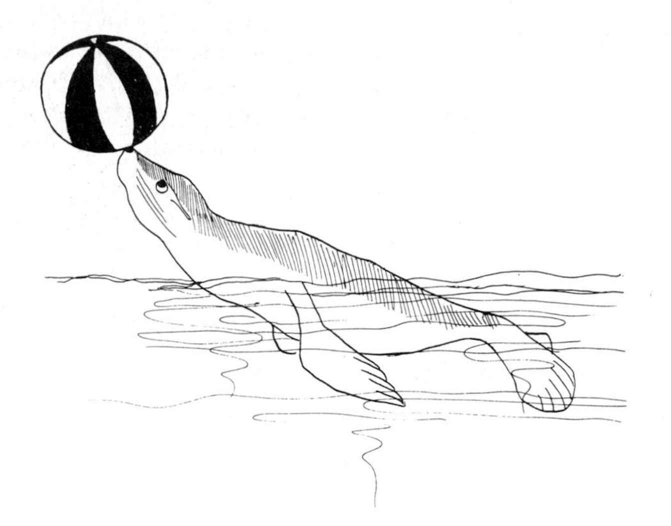

adj.
The seal is a *playful* swimmer.
adv.
The seal swims *playfully*.

Rhetorical Focus: ***Description, Exemplification***

Grammar Focus: ***Adjectives and Adverbs***

Exercise:

Describe a place in your country that a person should visit. The title should be the name of the place. Look at the example below. Try to write just eight sentences. Use *adjectives* and *adverbs.* Please write on a separate sheet of paper.

Example:

Title: The Public Market

Introduction: I. The Public Market is an interesting place to see in Boston.

Body:
A. Good restaurants
B. Different stores
C. Artistic people

Conclusion: The Boston Public Market is a nice place to spend the day.

The Public Market

The Public Market is an interesting place to see in Boston. One reason is that there are many good restaurants there with a variety of foods. People can eat inexpensive food without waiting in line. Another reason to see the market is the different stores. There are all kinds of clothes, foods, plants, jewelry and crafts to find there. Finally, the market is full of artistic people who work skillfully. They make and sell beautiful things to the people. The Boston Public Market is a nice place to spend the day.

Rhetorical Focus: ***Description Exemplification***

Grammar Focus: ***Adjectives and Adverbs***

Exercise:

Think about someone you know and talk about that person's profession. Discuss things such as how they work or what kind of workers they are. Make sure to use *adjectives and adverbs* and to limit your composition to about eight sentences. Please use your own paper.

Example:

Title: The Dentist

Introduction: I. Although it is not easy, my brother-in-law is a good dentist because he works very hard and tries to do his job well.

Body:
A. Patience
B. Knowledge
C. Concentration

Conclusion: In short, it is nice to have a good dentist in the family.

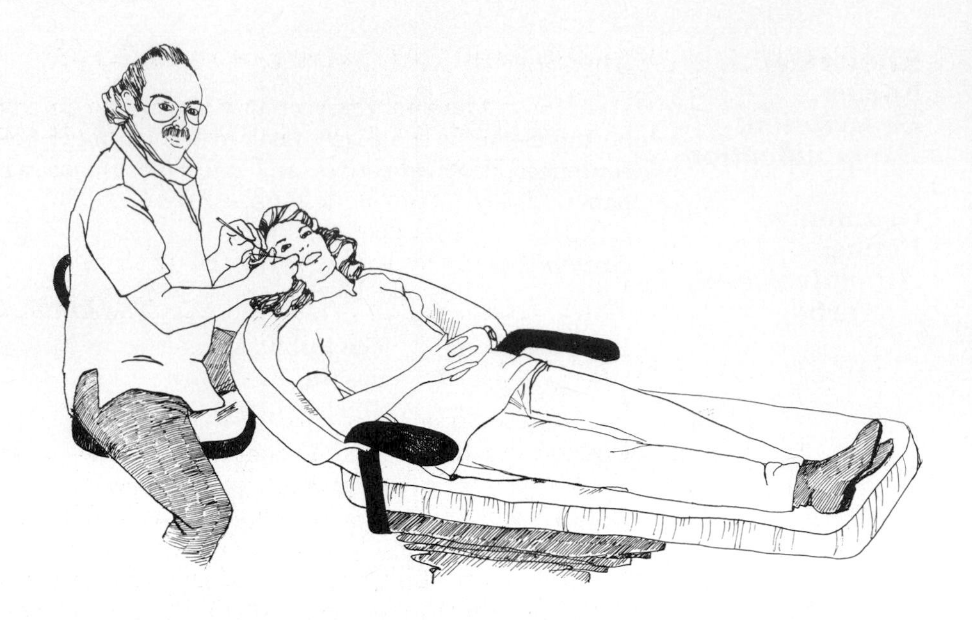

The Dentist

Although it is not easy, my brother-in-law is a good dentist because he works very hard and tries to do his job well. Patience, for instance, is an important quality for all dentists, since people feel afraid and do unusual things when they visit the dentist. For this reason, my brother-in-law is calm and never behaves impatiently with his patients. Besides that, it is necessary to study diligently in order to become a competent professional. My brother-in-law learned a lot in dental school and always applies his knowledge fully. Moreover, in order to do a good job, dentists must think about their work seriously. Accordingly, my brother-in-law always pays complete attention to his work; therefore, he does his job successfully. In short, it is nice to have a good dentist in the family.

GRAMMAR REVIEW: *ADVERBIALS OF PURPOSE*

> There are three answers to questions beginning with *Why?*
> *Example:*
> *Why* are you going shopping?
> 1. for a pair of shoes
> 2. (in order) to buy a pair of shoes
> 3. because I need a pair of shoes

ADVERBIALS IN CONTEXT

1. *for + noun or noun phrase*
   He went to the department store *for some shoes.*
   They were in Las Vegas *for a vacation.*
2. *(in order) to + verb (infinitive) + noun phrase*
   He went to the department store *in order to buy a pair of shoes.*
   He went to the department store *to buy a pair of shoes.*
   They went to Las Vegas *to gamble* during their vacation.
3. *because + longer explanations*
   He went to the department store *because he needed a pair of shoes.*
   They were in Las Vegas *because they wanted to take a vacation.*

GRAMMAR REVIEW: *ADVERBIALS OF MEANS AND INSTRUMENT*

1. *Communication* (by + noun):
How do you communicate? *How* do people communicate?

by phone	by T.V.
by telegram	by telestar
by telex	by computer
by cable	by C.B.
by letter	by sign language
by radio	by body language
by air mail	by smoke signals

ADVERBIALS IN CONTEXT

I communicate with my family *by phone* and *by mail.*
The president communicates with the American people *by T.V. and radio.*
Deaf people communicate *by (using) sign language.*

2. *Transportation* (by + noun):
How do you get to school? *How* do people travel?

by bus	by motorcycle	on foot
by car	by bike	
by taxi	by horse	
by train	by camel	
by plane	by mule	
by helicopter	by donkey	

ADVERBIALS IN CONTEXT

In the past people traveled *by horse.*
He arrived *by train.*
She came *on foot.*

3. *Tools, Utensils, Instruments* (with + noun):
*How** do you eat soup? *How* do you put in a nail?

with a key	with (her) foot
with a fork	with (his) thumb
with a knife	with (my) fingers
with a spoon	with (my) fist
with a screwdriver	
with a hammer	
with a shovel	
with an axe	

ADVERBIALS IN CONTEXT

I eat my dinner *with a fork and knife.*
She is putting the nail in the wall *with a hammer.*
He opened the door *with a key.*

**Note: The question How?* can also be answered with *adverbs of manner. Example: How* does he drive his new car? He drives his new car *quickly.*

Rhetorical Focus: ***Cause and Effect, Chronological Order***

Grammar Focus: ***Adverbials of Purpose***

Exercise:

Discuss the reasons *why* you did something in a logical, *cause and effect* manner. Use *adverbials of purpose* and try to write eight sentences. Please write on a separate sheet of paper.

Example:

Title: Why I Came to the West Coast

Introduction: I. There are different reasons that I left home to come to the West Coast.

A. Travel

Body: B. Change

C. Friends

Conclusion: I am happy that I came west though I still miss many things about the East Coast.

Why I Came to the West Coast

There are different reasons that I left home to come to the West Coast. One reason for leaving was because I like to travel. Hence, by coming here, I was able to see many new places. However, that wasn't cause enough for me to move. Another reason I came here was for a change, i.e., I wanted to have new experiences and a different routine. The third reason I took a trip out West was to visit friends. Many of my good friends from home were living here. I am happy that I came west though I still miss many things about the East Coast.

Rhetorical Focus: ***Process, Chronological Order***

Grammar Focus: ***Modals, Adverbials***

Exercise:

Explain how something is done in a *process* form. Each step of the process should be explained in *chronological* or *time sequence*. Make sure to use *modals and adverbials of manner, means, instrument, and purpose*. Write the process in eight sentences, and use your own paper.

Example:

Title: How to Learn English

Introduction: I. In order to learn English it is important to do three things.

A. Study

Body: B. Speak

C. Read

Conclusion: It is difficult to learn a language; accordingly, a person can learn English very fast by doing these things.

How to Learn English

In order to learn English it is important to do three things. First, students must study very seriously without wasting time. Indeed, good English students are hard workers. Second, language learners should speak English carefully. In other words, they had better not become lazy by speaking their native languages. Third, students of English ought to read many different books. Reading is good for vocabulary and is useful for improving comprehension. It is difficult to learn a language; accordingly, a person can learn English very fast by doing these things.

GRAMMAR REVIEW: *MODALS—MUST, HAVE TO, SHOULD, OUGHT TO, HAD BETTER*

MODALS: MUST

Affirmative		*Negative*		*Interrogative*		
I		I			I	
She		She			she	
He		He			he	
It	must work.	It	must not work.	(How) Must	it	work?
We		We	mustn't		we	
You		You			you	
They		They			they	

MODALS: HAVE TO

Affirmative			*Negative*			*Interrogative*		
I	have to		I	do not don't		Do	I	
She			She				she	
He	has to		He	does not doesn't		Does	he	
It		work.	It		have to work.		it	have to work?
We	have to		We				we	
You			You	do not don't		Do	you	
They			They				they	

MODALS: SHOULD

Affirmative		*Negative*		*Interrogative*		
I		I			I	
She		She			she	
He		He			he	
It	should arrive.	It	should not arrive.	(When) Should	it	arrive?
We		We	shouldn't		we	
You		You			you	
They		They			they	

*MODALS** IN CONTEXT

The English teacher says:
You *have to* come on time. You *must not* be late to class.
You *must* speak only English. You *don't have to* speak your native language.
You *must* try to use what you learn in class, outside of class.
You *mustn't* be afraid to speak English.
You *have to* meet English-speaking people and practice.

**See Appendix I for a review of modals.*

MODALS: OUGHT TO		
Affirmative	***Negative***	***Interrogative***
I / She / He / It / We / You / They } ought to wait.	I / She / He / It / We / You / They } ought not to wait.	(Why) Should { I / she / he / it / we / you / they } wait?

MODALS: HAD BETTER		
Affirmative	***Negative***	***Interrogative***
I / She / He / It / We / You / They } had better wait.	I / She / He / It / We / You / They } had better not wait.	(Why) Had (not) { I / she / he / it / we / you / they } better wait?

MODALS IN CONTEXT

Advice: Pedro has many problems and Pierre gives him advice.

Rhetorical Focus: ***Process, Classification***

Grammar Focus: ***Modals—Should, Shouldn't***

Exercise:

Your best American friend is going to your country and needs your advice about how to prepare for life there. Write no more than eight sentences about what your friend *should* do. Please use a separate sheet of paper.

Example:

Title: Dos and Don'ts in the United States

Introduction: I.

The United States is different from home, and there are some things foreigners should do and others they should not do there.

Body:

A. People
B. Customs
C. Laws

Conclusion: In conclusion, when in Rome do as the Romans do.

<u>*Dos and Don'ts in the United States*</u>

The United States is different from home, and there are some things foreigners should do and others they should not do. As an illustration, American people are friendly, but private. Then, visitors to the United States should respect Americans' privacy and time to be alone. Another reason to be careful is that Americans' customs differ from the customs of other countries, i.e., foreigners should not expect American people to have the same traditions as those in other countries. Every place has its own rules. In like manner, American laws are not the same. Therefore, tourists should understand the laws of a country before they make bad mistakes. In conclusion, when in Rome, do as the Romans do.

Rhetorical Focus: *Process, Chronological Order*

Grammar Focus: *Modals—Should, Had Better, Ought To*

Exercise:

Imagine that you are a student advisor in a school and one of the students comes to you with a problem. What kind of advice will you give? Try to use the modals *should, should not, ought to, ought not to, had better, had better not, can, cannot, could, could not.* Write your advice in eight sentences if possible. Please use your own paper.

Example:

Title: The Students' Problem

Introduction: I. Students can avoid problems in the United States if they are careful.

Body:
A. Immigration
B. Studies
C. Laws

Conclusion: In conclusion, it is easy for foreign students to have a good life in the United States if they are not careless.

<u>*The Students' Problem*</u>

Students can avoid problems in the United States if they are careful. First, they should check all of their papers with immigration, and they had better not wait a long time before they do that. Furthermore, they should renew their passports; otherwise, they will have difficulties when their passports expire. Next, foreign students ought to study hard; i.e., they cannot be lazy. In other words, they should try to do their best in school. Finally, people from other countries had better respect American laws. They ought not to do anything illegal in this country. In conclusion, it is easy for foreign students to have a good life in the United States if they are not careless.

GRAMMAR REVIEW: *OBJECT PRONOUNS*

Subjects:	***Objects:***
I	Me
She	Her
He	Him
It	It
We	Us
You	You
They	Them

OBJECT PRONOUNS IN CONTEXT

My friend wants to visit *me* in this country. I sent *him* information about U.S. immigration. I told *him* the rules. He is going to bring *me* his important papers. I will take *him* to the immigration office. They always ask foreigners a lot of questions. My friend will answer *them.* He will give *them* his papers. Then I will make dinner *for him.* I will explain the customs and describe the food *to him.*

Rhetorical Focus: *Narration, Chronological Order*

Grammar Focus: *Direct and Indirect Objects*

Exercise:

Imagine that a good friend of yours is sick, getting married, or leaving your country. Use the *direct and indirect object verb patterns* to describe what you did when you saw your friend. You need to write only eight sentences on a separate sheet of paper.

Example:

Title: A Visit to the Hospital

Introduction: I. My good friend was sick, and I went to visit her in the hospital.

A. News

Body: B. Gifts

C. Help

Conclusion: I hope my friend felt better after my visit.

A Visit to the Hospital

My good friend was sick, and I went to visit her in the hospital. First, I told her some funny stories about our friends. Next, she asked me many questions about school. In addition, I brought my friend some food and cake that people made for her. Later, I gave her a book from the teacher. After, she felt cold, so I closed the window for her. Then, I opened the bottle of medicine that the doctor prescribed for her. I hope my friend felt better after my visit.

Rhetorical Focus: ***Narration, Chronological Order***

Grammar Focus: ***Direct and Indirect Objects***

Exercise:

Describe a party you once had that you didn't expect to have. Try to use *direct and indirect objects* and write about eight sentences on your own paper.

Example:

Title: The Surprise Party

Introduction: I. Last year my friends gave me a wonderful surprise that I will never forget.

Body:
A. Dinner
B. Cake
C. Presents

Conclusion: In short, birthdays are pleasant when friends do nice things for each other.

The Surprise Party

Last year my friends gave me a wonderful surprise that I will never forget. In the afternoon, they invited me to their house in order to play a game. However, before I arrived, my friends made a wonderful dinner for me. Then, they asked me to go to a movie with them. Suddenly, they brought me a beautiful cake for my birthday. After we happily ate the cake, they offered me some presents. I did not open the presents until they wanted me to. In short, birthdays are pleasant when friends do nice things for each other.

GRAMMAR REVIEW: *TOO, ENOUGH, VERY*

Too	means *excessive, more than enough.*
Enough	means *sufficient, just right.*
Very	means *a lot, to a high level.*

TOO, ENOUGH, AND VERY IN CONTEXT

Those people are *very* rich. They live in a big house with a swimming pool. There are five different cars in their garage; for instance, a Rolls Royce, a Mercedes, a Cadillac, a Ferrari, and a Porsche.

That student was driving *too* fast. The speed limit is fifty-five miles per hour, and he was driving seventy-five miles per hour. That is *too* fast to be legal.

Those women are eighteen. In this state, they are old *enough* to drink alcohol. In that state, they are *too* young to drink because the law says that people must be twenty-one. However, they are *very* happy because they are old *enough* to vote in the United States.

Rhetorical Focus: *Narration, Description*

Grammar Focus: *Too, Enough, Very*

Exercise:

Remember an experience you have had where there was either an excess (too much) of something or a deficiency (not enough) of that thing. Make an effort to use *too, enough* and *very* and to limit yourself to eight sentences if possible. Please use a separate sheet of paper.

Example:

Title: The Foreign Students' Party

Introduction: I. The students at school had a very nice celebration at the end of the term.

A. Food

Body: B. Music

C. Drink

Conclusion: The people who came to the party ate too much; nevertheless, they had an enjoyable time.

The Foreign Students' Party

The students at school had a very nice celebration at the end of the term. All the people brought a special dish from their country, e.g., sushi, kapsa, enchiladas, curry, and arepas. When everyone arrived, there was too much food to eat. In addition, they brought different cassettes and records from all over the world. Unfortunately, there was not enough time to listen to all of them. On top of that, the weather was too hot for warm drinks, so everybody drank cold beverages. Nobody had too much to drink. The people who came to the party ate too much; nevertheless, they had an enjoyable time.

Rhetorical Focus: ***Narration, Classification***

Grammar Focus ***Too, Enough, Very***

Exercise:

Remember a situation in your life when you felt uncomfortable or out of place because you were not the right age, correctly dressed, properly prepared, or well-informed about where you were going. Use *too, enough,* and *very* to emphasize your situation and limit yourself to eight sentences if possible. Please write on your own paper.

Example:

Title: Visiting Elementary School

Introduction: I. When I went back to visit my elementary school, I felt very strange.

A. Age

Body: B. Size

C. Teachers

Conclusion: I waited too long to go back and visit my first school; as a result, I felt very out of place when I finally did.

Visiting Elementary School

When I went back to visit my elementary school, I felt very strange. First, I was too old to be there. In fact, I was old enough to be the students' mother! Second, everything in the school was very small, and I was too large to use some things. The water fountain was too low for me to drink from; besides that, I was not small enough to sit in the chairs. Third, I did not recognize a lot of teachers, because my teachers became too old to teach. A lot of the new teachers were young enough to be my classmates. I waited too long to go back and visit my first school; as a result, I felt very out of place when I finally did.

GRAMMAR REVIEW: *COMPARISONS*

Sameness (Equality)	*Difference* (Inferiority)	*Difference* (Superiority)
noun the same *size* as similar to like **adj./adv.** as *tall/quickly* as	**noun** isn't the same *size* as **adj.** isn't as *tall* as **adv.** doesn't go as *quickly* **adj./noun** less *intelligent/money* than **noun** fewer *dollars* than **noun** worse *results* than	**noun** isn't the same *size* as **adj.** isn't as *small/slow* as **adj./noun** more *intelligent/money* than **noun** better *results* than

Spelling Rules for One-Syllable Comparisons and Superlatives*			
Add -er or *-est* to most words of one syllable.	*Add* only *-r,* or *-st* if a word ends in *-e.*	*Double the consonant* before adding *-er* or *-est* if a one syllable word ends with a single vowel followed by a single consonant.	*Change y* to *i* and *add -er* or *-est* if a word of one or more syllable ends in *-y.*
Examples: tall taller than the tallest of	*Examples:* nice nicer than the nicest of	*Examples:* red redder than the reddest of	*Examples:* lazy lazier than the laziest of

COMPARISONS IN CONTEXT

The Eiffel Tower is not *the same height as* the Empire State Building.
French is *similar to* Spanish.
Identical twins look *alike.*
My country is *different from* your country.
Rich people have *more money than* poor people.

Rhetorical Focus: *Comparison and Contrast*

Grammar Focus: *Comparisons*

Exercise:

Compare two people that you know. They can be friends, teachers, family members, or classmates. Try to use the *comparisons* from class and write a good paragraph of about eight sentences. Try the **AB AB AB** approach on a separate sheet of paper.

Example:

Title: My Two Friends

Introduction: I. My two friends have similar and different characteristics, such as appearance, personality, and hobbies.

Body:
A. Appearance
B. Personality
C. Hobbies

Conclusion: Wendy and Lisa are friends; for this reason, other people like to compare them.

**See Appendix J for a list of comparisons and superlatives.*

Two Friends

My two friends have similar and different characteristics, such as appearance, personality and hobbies. Wendy is short and blonde. In contrast, Lisa is taller than Wendy, and Lisa's hair is much darker and curlier than Wendy's. Wendy is the shy type and doesn't talk loudly when other people are there. On the other hand, Lisa is more outgoing than Wendy and likes to speak more. Both Lisa and Wendy enjoy doing different things, and they do them well. For instance, Wendy is a folk dancer, and she dances more gracefully than Lisa, but Lisa can play racquetball better than Wendy. Wendy and Lisa are friends; for this reason, other people like to compare them.

Rhetorical Focus: *Comparison and Contrast*

Grammar Focus: *Comparisons*

Exercise:

Compare and contrast two places or things that you are familiar with by using the *er* and *more . . . than, less . . . than* forms. Please limit yourself to about eight sentences, and use a separate sheet of paper.

Example:

Title: Different Seasons on Two Coasts

Introduction: I. There are similarities and differences between the seasonal changes in different American cities.

Body
- A. Winter
- B. Summer
- C. Spring and fall

Conclusion: While I like autumn and spring better in Philadelphia than in Portland, summer and winter are much milder and more comfortable in Portland.

Different Seasons on Two Coasts

There are similarities and differences between the seasonal changes in different American cities. For example, winter is colder on the East Coast, and there is more snow than on the west coast. In fact, Portland, a northwestern city, has less snow and a warmer temperature than northeastern Philadelphia although Portland is further north. Conversely, Philadelphia is more humid and hotter than Portland in the summer, but the days are sunnier. Portland is less uncomfortable, yet it is rainier and cloudier than Philadelphia during the summer. In addition, autumn and spring are more beautiful in Philadelphia than in Portland because the colors of the leaves and flowers change more drastically, and the weather remains more moderate. Portland's changes are less noticeable during these seasons, and the colors are less dramatic. While I like autumn and spring better in Philadelphia than in Portland, summer and winter are much milder and more comfortable in Portland.

GRAMMAR REVIEW: *SUPERLATIVES AND COMPARISONS*

Inferiority	the least (_____) of
	the fewest (_____) of
	the worst (_____) of
Superiority	the most (_____) of
	the best (_____) of

SUPERLATIVES AND COMPARISONS IN CONTEXT

Gloria is *thinner than* Dave.
Dave is *heavier than* Gloria, Pam, and Bob. He is *the heaviest of* all.
Bob is *shorter than* Dave, Gloria, and Pam. He is *the shortest of* all.
Pam has *less money than* Gloria.
Gloria is *the richest.*
Bob's shoes are *the newest of all.*
Gloria has *the whitest shoes of all.*
Bob's pants have *fewer stripes than* Gloria's.
Gloria's stripes are *the thickest of all.* She is *the best* dresser.
Bob is *the youngest.* He has *the fewest* teeth.
Dave is *the oldest.*
Gloria has a good smile. It is *better than* Dave's.
Pam has *the best* smile of all.
Dave has *the worst* eyesight of all.
Gloria is *the most beautiful* of all.
Dave is *the hairiest of all.*
Bob is *the least talkative of the family.*
Pam is *the most cheerful of all.* She is *the happiest of the family.*

Rhetorical Focus: ***Narrative***

Grammar Focus: ***Superlatives***

Exercise:

Discuss the best, worst, funniest, saddest, happiest experience you can remember. Make sure to use *superlative forms* and try to limit yourself to eight sentences if possible. Please write on a separate sheet of paper.

Example:

Title: The Most Frightening Experience I Have Had

Introduction: I. My most frightening experience happened when I was sixteen and traveling overseas for the first time.

Body:
A. No ticket
B. No possessions
C. No money

Conclusion: It was the scariest experience of my life when it happened; nevertheless, since then, it has become my most enjoyable story to tell.

The Most Frightening Experience I Have Had

My most frightening experience happened when I was sixteen and traveling overseas for the first time. While I was at the airport in Europe, the clerk told me that my airplane ticket was not valid; consequently, I couldn't use it. That was my most horrible moment! After I waited twelve of my most frustrating hours, the airlines put me on one flight, but sent all my belongings on another. Of all the passengers, I had the smallest number of things to carry. Moreover, I had very little money because I had to spend most of it on my new plane ticket. My wallet was probably the lightest of all. It was the scariest experience of my life when it happened; nevertheless, since then, it has become my most enjoyable story to tell.

Rhetorical Focus: ***Comparison and Contrast, Classification, Cause and Effect***

Grammar Focus: ***Superlatives***

Exercise:

Talk about your favorite ____________ or your least favorite ________. Make sure to use the *superlative forms* from class. Try not to write more than eight sentences if possible, and use your own paper.

Example:

Title: My Favorite Car

Introduction: I. The Trans Am is my favorite car for many reasons.

A. Appearance

Body: B. Speed

C. Strength

Conclusion: To conclude, there are many cars on the road, but the best one of all is the Pontiac Trans Am.

My Favorite Car

The Trans Am is my favorite car for many reasons. First of all, this car is the most beautiful car of all because it is shinier and more colorful than the others. It looks better than other cars because it has a picture on the hood—a phoenix. Not only that, the Trans Am is faster than most other cars. It is also the best car for winning a race. In addition, the Trans Am is one of the strongest American cars. It is less dangerous than other cars because it has harder metal on the outside and its engine is the most powerful of all. To conclude, there are many cars on the road, but the best one of all is the Pontiac Trans Am.

GRAMMAR REVIEW: *PRESENT PERFECT*

Affirmative			*Negative*			*Interrogative*		
I (I've)	have	gone.	I	have not / haven't	gone.	Have	I	gone?
She (She's) / He (He's) / It (It's)	has		She / He / It	has not / hasn't		(Where) Has	she / he / it	
We (We've) / You (You've) / They (They've)	have		We / You / They	have not / haven't		Have	we / you / they	

PRESENT PERFECT IN CONTEXT

I *haven't seen* my elementary school friends for many years. Nevertheless, my friend *Brad has lived* in my neighborhood since then. *He hasn't gotten* married yet. On the other hand, his *sister has already had* two children. *We have not spoken* since 1970. *It has been* a long time since elementary school. *My friends have changed* in many ways. What *have they done* since we were children?

GRAMMAR REVIEW: *PRESENT PERFECT CONTINUOUS*

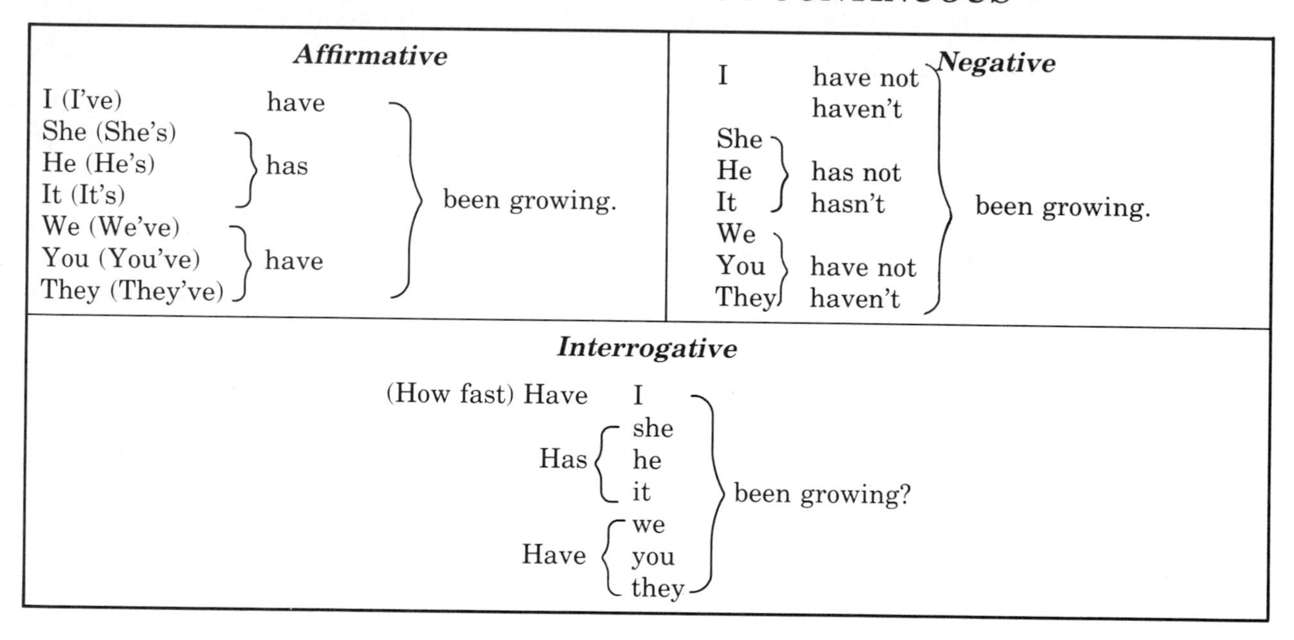

Affirmative			*Negative*		
I (I've)	have	been growing.	I	have not / haven't	been growing.
She (She's) / He (He's) / It (It's)	has		She / He / It	has not / hasn't	
We (We've) / You (You've) / They (They've)	have		We / You / They	have not / haven't	

Interrogative		
(How fast) Have	I	been growing?
Has	she / he / it	
Have	we / you / they	

PRESENT PERFECT CONTINUOUS IN CONTEXT

I *have been teaching* for many years.
She *has been driving* all day long.
He *has been studying* since this morning.
It *has been ringing* continuously.
We *haven't been waiting* for a long time.
You *haven't been working* for the last month, have you?
They *have been traveling* since last summer.

PRESENT PERFECT VS. *PRESENT PERFECT CONTINUOUS* IN CONTEXT

Yona: It *has been raining* all week. Will it ever stop?

Eddie: I don't know. It *has snowed* a lot this winter, but it *hasn't rained* like this all year long.

Yona: We *have had* terrible weather, *haven't* we?

Eddie: Yes! I *have been dreaming* about sunshine and beaches. The other people in my band are on vacation in Hawaii now.

Yona: How nice! *Have* you *received* any postcards from them?

Eddie: No, I *haven't*. But I *have been checking* my mailbox every day.

Yona: *Have* they *called* you yet?

Eddie: Not since I *have been* home. The telephone *has rung* several times today, but the calls *haven't been* for me.

Yona: Maybe they *have been trying* to call you, but the lines *have been* busy because of the storm.

Eddie: That's very possible.

Yona: Listen. The phone *has been ringing* for a few seconds. You should answer it.

Eddie: That's right. Nobody else is home. It may be my friends. I *have been waiting* to hear from them.

Yona: Please send them my regards.

Rhetorical Focus: *Comparison and Contrast, Classification*

Grammar Focus: *Present Perfect*

Exercise:

Discuss how your life *has changed* since you have been in the United States. Try to limit yourself to only eight sentences if possible. Please use your own paper.

Example:

Title: How I Have Changed

Introduction: I. I have changed in many ways since I came to the United States.

A. Clothes

Body: B. Food

C. Music

Conclusion: I have developed new tastes and learned different things because of my visit to this country.

How I Have Changed

I have changed in many ways since I came to the United States. As an illustration, before I came here, I wore my country's traditional clothes. However, since I arrived, I have bought and worn typical American styles. What is more, in my country, I always ate what my mother prepared for me. In this country, on the other hand, I have learned to cook for myself, and I have eaten interesting foods. When I was home, I liked to listen to all kinds of music, but I could not go to many concerts. Here, in contrast, I have gone to concerts very often and I have heard jazz, rock 'n roll, and folk music. I have developed new tastes and learned different things because of my visit to this country.

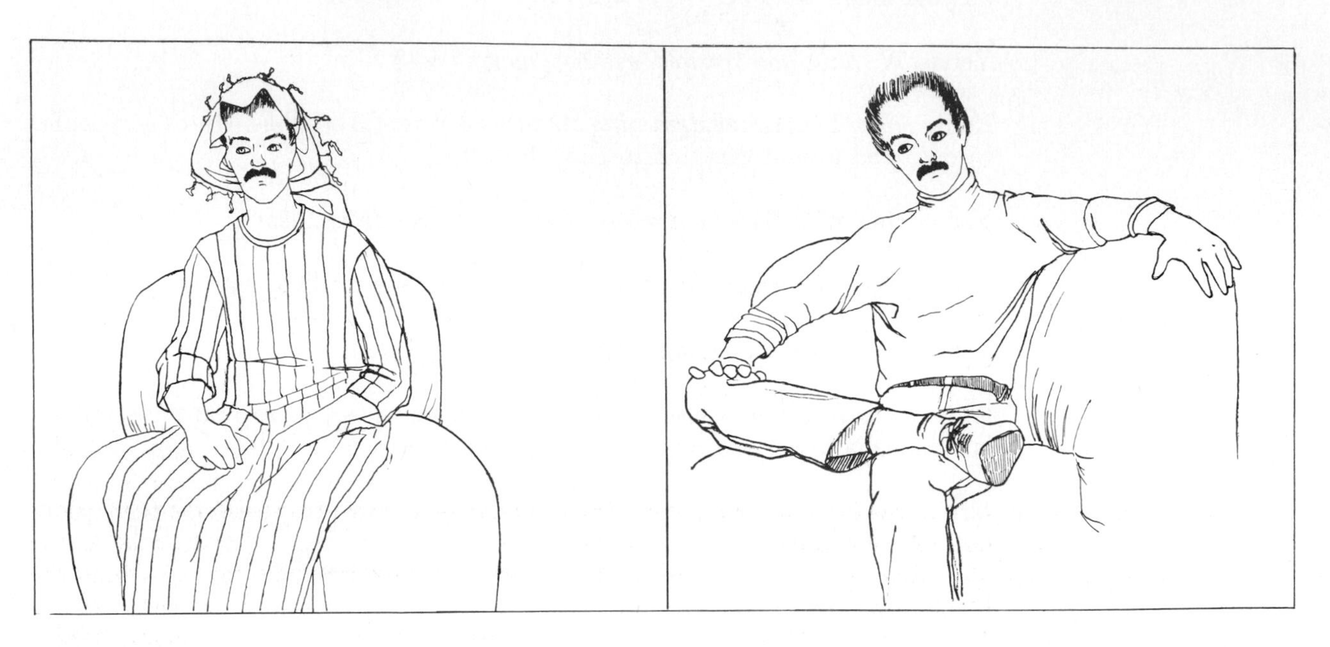

Rhetorical Focus: ***Narration, Description***

Grammar Focus: ***Present Perfect (Continuous)***

Exercise:

Imagine that you are a news reporter on television in your country and a major event has just taken place. Report the news to your audience in about eight sentences. Make sure to use *present perfect* in your news broadcast. Please write on a separate sheet of paper.

Example:

Title: The Volcano

Introduction: I. Mt. St. Helens, a volcano in the state of Washington, has just erupted again.

Body:
- A. Smoke
- B. Ash
- C. Lava

Conclusion: As a result, scientists have been very surprised by the activities of this strange volcano.

The Volcano

Mount St. Helens, a volcano in the state of Washington, has just erupted again. Consequently, people have seen a lot of smoke in the air. Besides that, a mushroom cloud has filled the sky. In the same way as before, western Washington has escaped the ash. This time the ash has fallen on eastern Washington. People have been expecting to see lava for quite some time. Luckily, the lava hasn't begun to flow yet. As a result, scientists have been very surprised by the activities of this strange volcano.

GRAMMAR REVIEW: *PASSIVE VOICE*

AFFIRMATIVE AND NEGATIVE		
Present and Present Continuous		
I	am (not)	accepted.
She, He, It	is	
We, You, They	are	

Past		
I, She, He, It	was (not)	accepted.
We, You, They	were	

Future	
I, She, He, It, We, You, They	will (not) be accepted.

Modals	
I can (not) be	accepted.
She must be	
He should be	
It has to be	
We could be	
You ought to be	
They had better be	

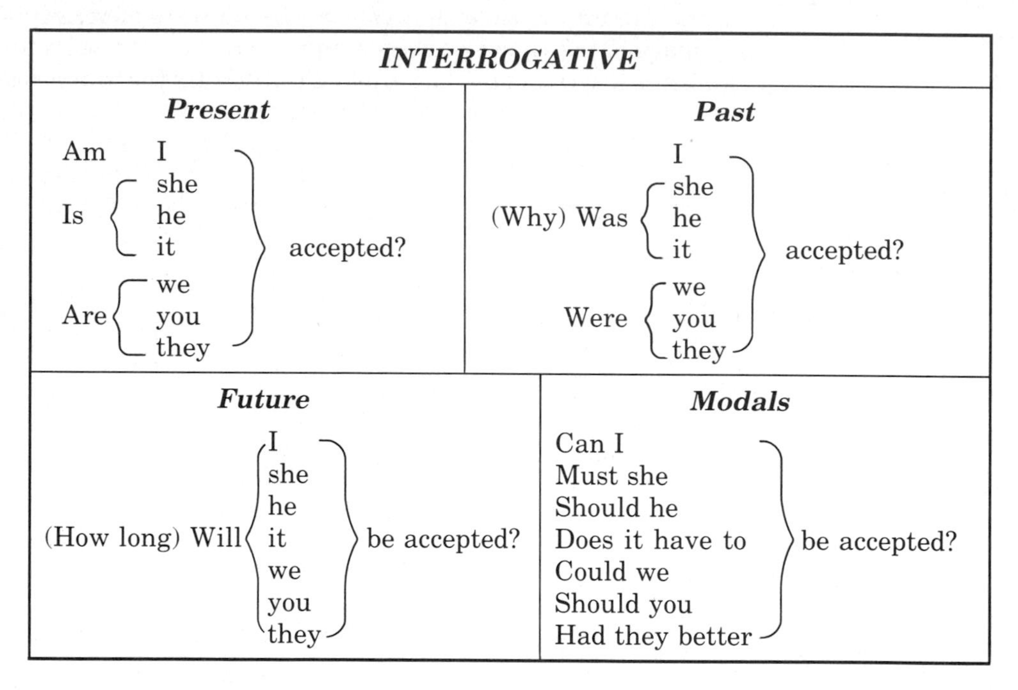

INTERROGATIVE		
Present		
Am	I	accepted?
Is	she, he, it	
Are	we, you, they	

Past		
(Why) Was	I, she, he, it	accepted?
Were	we, you, they	

Future		
(How long) Will	I, she, he, it, we, you, they	be accepted?

Modals	
Can I	be accepted?
Must she	
Should he	
Does it have to	
Could we	
Should you	
Had they better	

PASSIVE VOICE IN CONTEXT

List of Rules for the Substitute Teacher:

1. English *must be spoken* in class. Native languages *should not be used.*
2. Smoking *is not permitted* in the building.
3. Food *should not be eaten* in class.
4. The plants *are watered* three times a week.
5. Tests *were given* last week.
6. Final exams *will be taken* at the end of the course.
7. Students *are being taught* grammar, conversation, reading, writing, and other skills.
8. Tapes and cassettes *can be found* in the language laboratory.

This list *was written* by the teacher. She *can be reached* at home.

Rhetorical Focus: ***Process, Chronological Order***

Grammar Focus: ***Passive Voice***

Exercise:

Describe a process or the *how* of something. Explain the process in correct *time order*. Make sure to use the *passive voice*. Use about eight sentences and *connectors of chronological sequence* for your process. Write on your own paper.

Example:

Title: How to Blow Bubbles

Introduction: I. It is not difficult to learn how to blow bubbles.

A. Chew

Body: B. Spread

C. Blow

Conclusion: When these steps are followed in correct order, it is easy and a lot of fun to blow bubbles.

How to Blow Bubbles

It is not difficult to learn how to blow bubbles. First, the bubble gum is placed in the mouth and chewed thoroughly. It must be chewed long enough to be softened. Then, the gum is ready to be spread. The tongue is placed inside the soft gum. Finally, the bubble can be made. Air is blown into the soft, spread gum, and the gum is changed into a large bubble. When these steps are followed in correct order, it is easy and a lot of fun to blow bubbles.

Rhetorical Focus: ***Process, Chronological Order***

Grammar Focus: ***Passive Voice***

Exercise:

Imagine that you are an exporter, and you want to send some of your country's products to another country. Discuss the things which can be found in your country. Try to write no more than eight sentences, and use your own paper.

Example:

Title: My Country's Specialties

Introduction: I. The United States is a big country where many things are sold.

A. Machinery

Body: B. Clothing

C. Food

Conclusion: To summarize, a variety of products is exported from the United States to other countries of the world.

My Country's Specialties

The United States is a big country where many things are sold. Technology is being developed here, so different kinds of machines are manufactured. Last year, for instance, many industrial machines were bought by other countries. In addition, many new clothes were made in the United States. The best clothing stores are found in the fashion center, New York City. Furthermore, different fruits and vegetables are grown in this country. Next year, this food will be sold to other countries. To summarize, a variety of products is exported from the United States to other countries of the world.

GRAMMAR REVIEW: *USED TO*

Affirmative	*Negative*	*Interrogative*
I / She / He / It / We / You / They } used to work.	I / She / He / It / We / You / They } didn't use to work.	(Why) Did { I / she / he / it / we / you / they } use to work?

USED TO IN CONTEXT

I *used to live* in a different city.
She *used to eat* with chopsticks.
She *didn't use to eat* with a fork and a knife.
He *used to watch* more television than now.
Did he *use to* read?
It *didn't use to* break down so often.
It *used to* work well.
We *didn't use to* wear jeans.
Did you *use to* drive in your country?
How *did* they *use to* travel?

Rhetorical Focus: ***Description***

Grammar Focus: ***Used to***

Exercise:

Write a paragraph about your daily routine when you were living in your country. You could discuss your family, your school, your childhood, your job, or anything you *used to* do regularly. Try to write no more than eight sentences. Please write on a separate sheet of paper.

Example:

Title: My Student Routine

Introduction: I. As a university student, I used to do some things on weekdays and other things on the weekends.

A. Study

Body: B. Work

C. Play

Conclusion: During my college days, I used to have different activities.

My Student Routine

As a university student, I used to do some things on weekdays and other things on the weekends. For example, from Monday through Friday I studied hard. I spent my time in class and at the library. In addition, I worked after class in the student cafeteria. However, I didn't use to study or work on Saturdays and Sundays. Instead, I had a good time with my friends. During my college days, I used to have different activities.

Rhetorical Focus:
Exemplification

Grammar Focus:
Used To

Exercise:

Write about something you *used to* do at one time that you don't do now. This could be because you are in a different place, you are a different age, you can't do that activity during this season, or you don't like to do what you used to do. Try not to write more than eight sentences. Please use your own paper.

Example:

Title: Before and Now

Introduction: I. I used to do things differently when I lived with my parents.

A. Expenses

Body: B. Transportation

C. Lodging

Conclusion: My life has changed since the time that I lived with my parents.

Before and Now

I used to do things differently when I lived with my parents. First, I didn't use to spend a lot of money. I lived with my parents, and they paid for rent and clothing. What's more, I never drove when I lived there. I always used to ride public transportation, such as the subway or the bus. Furthermore, I didn't use to live in a house. On the contrary, I used to live in an apartment with my parents and sister. My life has changed since the time that I lived with my parents.

GRAMMAR REVIEW: *REAL CONDITIONALS*

Present Affirmative

IF CLAUSE RESULT CLAUSE

If + present form, present form or polite request:

Habit	*If* the alarm clock *rings,* she *wakes* up.
Request	*If* you *go* downtown, *please buy* me a newspaper.
Generalization	*If* you *are* rich, you *are* happy.

Present Negative

IF CLAUSE RESULT CLAUSE

If + (negative) present form, (negative) present form *or* ***(negative) polite request:***

Habit	*If* the alarm clock *doesn't ring,* she *sleeps.*
Request	*If* you *finish* early, *don't forget* to call them.
Generalization	*If* you *aren't* rich, you *aren't* happy.
	If it's *not* one thing, it *is* another.

Future Affirmative

IF CLAUSE RESULT CLAUSE

If + present form, future.

If we *have* enough money, we *will travel* next summer.
If we *have* enough money, we *are going to travel* next summer.

Future Negative

IF CLAUSE RESULT CLAUSE

If + (negative) present form, (negative) future form.

If he *doesn't arrive* tonight, I *won't go* to the airport.
If he *doesn't arrive* tonight, I *am not going to go* to the airport.

REAL CONDITIONALS IN CONTEXT

If they *receive* a scholarship, they *will study* in another country. *If* they *study* in the United States, they *will learn* English. *If* they *learn* English well, they *will get* a better job when they return. *If* they *don't,* they *will find* a job that doesn't require English. *If* students *work* hard, they *don't have* many problems.

Rhetorical Focus: *Exemplification, Classification*

Grammar Focus: *Future Real Conditionals*

Exercise:

Write about some superstitions, customs, or beliefs that are popular in your country. Try to write no more than eight sentences, and use your own paper.

Example:

Title: Superstitions

Introduction: I. It is interesting to see that different countries have similar ideas about good and bad luck.

A. Plants

Body: B. Animals

C. Things

Conclusion: Some people believe in superstitions, other people do not; nevertheless, the same ideas can be found around the world.

Superstitions

It is interesting to see that different countries have similar ideas about good and bad luck. For instance, in Japan you will have good luck if you find a four leaf clover. Similarly, this plant will bring good luck in other countries of Asia, North and South America, and Europe. On the other hand, black animals such as crows and cats are bad luck in many countries. However, if you have rabbits' feet and horses' shoes, you will be lucky. Finally, you will have many years of bad luck in most countries if you break a mirror. Furthermore, if you want good luck, you will not walk under a ladder. Some people believe in superstitions, other people do not; nevertheless, the same ideas can be found around the world.

Rhetorical Focus: ***Exemplification Definition***

Grammar Focus: ***Present Real Conditionals***

Exercise:

Write about some habits that you have that you always do. It's not necessary to write more than eight sentences. Please use a separate sheet of paper.

Example:

Title: Habits

Introduction: I. Most people have habits that are difficult to break.

Body:
- A. Sleeping
- B. Smoking
- C. Eating

Conclusion: In short, everybody has habits, and if it's not one thing, it's another.

Habits

Most people have habits that are difficult to break. For instance, my friend wakes up late if he doesn't set his alarm clock. In addition, if he falls asleep on his back, he always snores. As another example of habit, my students smoke every time they have a break. If they don't have a cigarette, they are nervous in class. Similarly, my cousin eats too much if he is worried or has free time. If he doesn't eat, his stomach makes loud noises. In short, everybody has habits, and if it's not one thing, it's another.

4 Suggestions For Expansion

Until now you have gone through the planning process of writing outlines for suggested eight-sentence paragraphs. You have also practiced applying your integrated knowledge of brainstorming, outlining, and refining and revising to the composing process by looking at model paragraphs.

You are beginning this chapter because you and your teacher have decided you are ready to write more *expanded* paragraphs. The chapter shows how the outline and suggested eight-sentence paragraph can be developed into an outlined three-paragraph composition with a suggested minimum of twenty-one sentences.

Model three-paragraph compositions are provided which combine grammar, organization, and creative content. At this point, you should be ready to apply what you have learned about one-paragraph compositions to longer pieces of writing. Your teacher will review new vocabulary with you. Then you will write your compositions on a separate sheet of paper.

You will also be presented with an expanded five-paragraph outline and composition which you can practice when you feel comfortable with one- and three- paragraph writing. Remember that paragraphs are *mini-compositions.* Just as one paragraph is made up of an introduction, body and conclusion, so is a longer composition. The following is a quick review of compositions or expanded paragraphs.

A *composition* (essay) usually has three, four or five paragraphs and a *title.* The title is given first and is always *capitalized.* The title describes what the composition is going to be about. Then there is an introductory paragraph, a body, and a concluding paragraph.

1. **The introductory paragraph** introduces (presents, shows, describes, illustrates, gives) an idea.
2. **The body** usually has one, two, or three paragraphs that support, describe, develop the idea (main point, topic, subject) of the introductory paragraph.
3. **The concluding paragraph** ends or finishes up the written discussion of the idea or subject that was introduced in the introductory paragraph.

Can you see that writing a paragraph is like writing a *miniature* composition?

MORE THAN ONE PARAGRAPH

Focus:
One- to Three- Paragraph Outline

You already know that it's quite simple to write an outline. When you understand a one-paragraph outline, it will be easy to write a three or more paragraph outline and, consequently, a three or more paragraph composition. Discuss with your teacher how the following examples show the relationship between a one-paragraph and three-paragraph outline. The three-paragraph outline is a development of the one-paragraph outline. Your teacher will point out the suggested sentence distribution for the actual composition as shown below.

*One-Paragraph Outline**		*Three-Paragraph Outline***	
Title:	Studying in Another Country	**Title:**	Studying in Another Country
Introduction:	I. There are many good reasons for people to study in a foreign country.	**Introduction:**	I. There are many good reasons for people to study in a foreign country.
		Transition:	↑ II. In another country, foreign students ↓ can learn about much more than just their major subject.
Body:	A. Language B. Culture C. People	**Body:**	A. Language B. Culture C. People
Conclusion:	People can broaden their experience and increase their knowledge by studying outside of their countries.	**Conclusion:**	People can broaden their experience and increase their knowledge by studying outside of their countries.

*This one-paragraph *composition* format suggests eight sentences distributed as the following chart indicates:

Introduction:	I.	1 sentence
Body:	A.	2 sentences
	B.	2 sentences
	C.	2 sentences
Conclusion:		1 sentence
		8 Total Sentences

**This three-paragraph *composition* format suggests thirteen sentences distributed as the following chart indicates:

Introduction:	I.	3 sentences
Transition:	II.	1 sentence
Body:	A.	2 sentences
	B.	2 sentences
	C.	2 sentences
Conclusion:	III.	3 sentences
		13 Total Sentences

Focus:
Expanding One Paragraph to Three Paragraphs

Your teacher will show you how this one-paragraph composition can be developed into a three-paragraph composition. This three-paragraph composition is similar to the one-paragraph composition except that it has a more developed introduction and conclusion with three sentences in each, in addition to a *transition* which connects the first paragraph to the second paragraph. The suggested total number of sentences in a three-paragraph composition is *thirteen* as opposed to *eight* in a one-paragraph composition. Your teacher will point out the relationship between the outlines and the compositions.

Studying in Another Country	*Studying in Another Country*
(1) There are many good reasons for people to study in a foreign country. (2) For example, it is a good opportunity for foreign students to learn a new language. (3) They can practice it every day. (4) In addition, people who study in another country are able to live in a different culture. (5) As a result, they will learn new customs and traditions. (6) Furthermore, foreigners will be in contact with new people. (7) They can develop relationships with international friends. (8) People can broaden their experience and increase their knowledge by studying abroad.	(1) There are many good reasons for people to study in a foreign country. (2) Students will be exposed to new situations. (3) Lots of knowledge can be gained from this type of experience. (4) In another country, foreign students can learn about much more than just their major subject. (5) For example, it is a good opportunity for them to learn a new language. (6) They will be able to practice it every day. (7) In addition, people who study in another country are able to live in a different culture. (8) As a result, they will learn new customs and traditions. (9) Furthermore, foreigners will be in contact with new people. (10) They can develop relationships with international friends. (11) People can broaden their experience and increase their knowledge by studying abroad. (12) Books will not be their only source of knowledge. (13) They will learn many things simply by experiencing the language, the culture and the people.

Focus:
Transition Practice

Exercise:

Fill in the sentences which will serve as *transitions* or topic sentences to the second paragraphs in the following three-paragraph outlines. They should be a *bridge* between the first and second paragraphs as well as an umbrella for the second paragraph.

Introduction: I. It was possible for me to study in my country, but I came to the United States.
↑
Transition: II. ______________________
↓
Body:
A. Travel
B. Language
C. People

Conclusion: III. I am happy that I came to the United States, but I still miss my country.

Introduction: I. There are several different ways of learning a new language.
↑
Transition: II. ______________________
↓
Body:
A. Listen
B. Speak
C. Write

Conclusion: III. A person can learn English very fast by doing these things.

Introduction: I. I have changed in many ways since I came to the United States.
↑
Transition: II. ______________________
↓
Body:
A. Clothes
B. Food
C. Music

Conclusion: III. I have developed new tastes and learned different things in this country.

Focus:
Three-Paragraph Outline Practice

Exercise:

Fill in the information for these three-paragraph outlines. With your teacher and classmates try to write three-paragraph compositions at the blackboard based on the outlines below.

Title: How I Have Changed
Introduction: I.
↑
Transition: II.
↓
Body:
A.
B.
C.

Conclusion: III.

Title:	Two People I Have Liked
Introduction:	I.
Transition:	II.
	A.
Body:	B.
	C.
Conclusion:	III.

Title:	News in My Country
Introduction:	I.
Transition:	II.
	A.
Body:	B.
	C.
Conclusion:	III.

COMPOSING THREE-PARAGRAPH COMPOSITIONS

Model three-paragraph compositions with outlines are provided for you to use as a source of guidance and support. The grammatical review and contexts are the same as those in Chapter 3. When you read these paragraphs before you write, keep in mind everything you have learned about brainstorming, outlining, organization, connectors, rhetorical devices, and revising. Don't be afraid to expand your writing.

You will have the opportunity to write even longer, five-paragraph compositions after you finish this three-paragraph practice.

Rhetorical Focus: ***Comparison and Contrast***

Grammar Focus: ***Comparisons****

Exercise:

Compare more than two people, places, or things that you are familiar with. Make sure to use all the *comparative forms* you have learned. Try to write only thirteen sentences as the model suggests. Your teacher will discuss difficult vocabulary with you. Please use your own paper.

Example:

Title: The Trio

Introduction: I. I knew three musicians who were sometimes similar, but other times extremely different.

↑

Transition: II. The trio had a few differences, but there were some major things in common.

↓

Body:

A. Physical appearance
B. Sense of humor
C. Musical ability

Conclusion: III. These three talented men spent a lot of time together, so they were always compared to each other.

The Trio

I knew three musicians who were sometimes similar, but other times extremely different. One played the saxophone, another played the drums, and the third played the piano. They always entertained their audiences with jokes and music.

The trio had a few differences, but there were major things in common. For instance, Kenny's hair was as blonde as Dave's, but Dave's beard was longer than Kenny's. Mike's hair color was different from that of the other two, his beard wasn't the same length as Dave's, and he was the shortest of the three. What's more, Mike, Kenny, and Dave had similar senses of humor, though Dave's was more like Kenny's and Mike didn't laugh at the same things as the other two. However, Mike's jokes were the funniest of all, and he smiled more than his friends. All three musicians were the most talented players in the area, and each one played differently than the other. They all loved music more than anything else in the world.

These three talented men spent a lot of time together, so they were always compared to each other by other people. Although they weren't exactly alike, they weren't too different. Each had his own special qualities.

*See page 121 for Grammar Review and Context: Comparisons. Also see Appendix J.

Rhetorical Focus: ***Comparison and Contrast***

Grammar Focus: ***Present Perfect****

Exercise:

Imagine that now you are living in the year 2020. Discuss what has happened in the world since 1986. Make sure to use the *present perfect tense*. Try to write no more than thirteen sentences as the model suggests. Your teacher will discuss difficult vocabulary with you. Please use your own paper.

Example:

Title: The Year 2020

Introduction: I. The world has changed radically since 1987.

Transition: II. Changes have occurred in many aspects of life.

Body:
A. Transportation
B. Food
C. Pollution

Conclusion: III. There have been other changes in our lives since 1987, but these have been the most significant.

The Year 2020

The world has changed radically since 1987. At that time, people worried about traffic in the cities, the limited supply of food, and the pollution of the environment. However, in recent years people have worked together in order to solve these problems.

Changes have occurred in many aspects of life. In the past, for example, there were too many cars and not enough public transportation. Since then, fast, efficient public transportation has become the major form of travel. Furthermore, twenty years ago people did not produce enough food because the land was not used wisely. In contrast, now people have learned better farming techniques that provide for everyone. In the 1980s, pollution was threatening the environment. Today, nations have adopted strict measures to control the causes of pollution.

*See page 126 for Grammar Review and Context: Present Perfect and Present Perfect Continuous Also see Appendix L for time words.

There have been many changes in our lives since 1987, but these have been the most significant. As a result of people's cooperation, the quality of life has improved. Nations have to work together to solve the problems of the future.

Rhetorical Focus: ***Description***

Grammar Focus: ***Present Perfect Continuous****

Exercise:

Write a three-paragraph composition about how your ________ has been changing recently. Make sure to use the *present perfect continuous.* Try to write only thirteen sentences as the model suggests. Please use your own paper.

Example:

Title: My Plant

Introduction: I. I have noticed that my plant has been changing recently.

Transition: II. My plant seems different every time I see it.

Body:
- A. Height
- B. Color
- C. Shape

Conclusion: III. I have been taking good care of my plant.

My Plant

I have noticed that my plant has been changing recently. It has matured into an adult plant and has become more beautiful. Its progress has been excellent.

My plant seems different every time I see it. It has been growing a lot lately. An illustration of this is that the plant has reached the top of the window. I have also become aware of a difference in color. In fact, the leaves of my plant have been changing from green to yellow and purple. In like manner, the shape of my plant has been changing. It has been getting a lot wider in the leaves and narrower in the stem.

I have been taking good care of my plant. It has been getting lots of sunshine and water all year long. Indeed, the results of my hard work have been very rewarding.

*See page 126 for Grammar Review and Context: Present Perfect and Present Perfect Continuous

Rhetorical Focus: ***Description, Process***

Grammar Focus: ***Modals****

Exercise:

Describe the process you went through in an emergency you have experienced. Make sure to use *modals* and to keep the experience in the *present tense* because you are to use *present modals.* Try to use only thirteen sentences, as the model suggests. Your teacher will discuss difficult vocabulary with you. Please use a separate sheet of paper.

Example:

Title: The Accident

Introduction: I. People must stay calm when they see an accident because many bad things might happen if they don't.

Transition: II. Many lives can be saved by remaining relaxed during a crisis.

Body:
A. Call
B. Help
C. Wait

Conclusion: III. It may not be easy to remain controlled in emergency situations, but it is absolutely necessary.

The Accident

People must stay calm when they see an accident because many bad things might happen if they don't. They may make a dangerous mistake because they are nervous. Somebody could die as a result of a situation like this.

Many lives can be saved by remaining relaxed during a crisis. Observers of an accident must not panic. They have to think clearly and call "911" for emergency assistance. The accident victim might or might not need help before the police and ambulance come. If the person needs help, an observer can apply some basic first aid. However, the best thing to do is to wait with the accident victim. Injured people should not be left alone because they may feel very afraid.

It may not be easy to remain controlled in emergency situations, but it is absolutely necessary. Accidents can happen at any time. People should be ready to help accident victims because lives could be saved.

Rhetorical Focus: ***Cause and Effect***

Grammar Focus: ***Passive Voice*****

Exercise:

Choose one product which you are interested in and write a commercial for it in the *passive voice.* Try to vary your tenses. Just write thirteen sentences to advertise your product. Your teacher will discuss difficult vocabulary with you. Make sure your readers understand *why* this product should be bought. Please use a separate sheet of paper.

Example:

Title: My Guitar

Introduction: I. Different guitars have been manufactured in the world, but my guitar has been bought by more people for many reasons.

*See pages 112 and 113 for Grammar Review and Context: Modals. Also see Appendix I.
**See page 130 for Grammar Review and Context: Passive Voice

Transition: II. This instrument is desired by all kinds of people because of its excellent quality.

Body:
A. Structure
B. Sound
C. Appearance

Conclusion: III. This style of guitar has been exported to a lot of different countries as a result of its superior quality.

My Guitar

Different guitars have been manufactured in the world, but my guitar has been bought by more people for many reasons. This guitar is used by many famous musicians because it is very reliable. It was designed by people who care about music.

This instrument is desired by all kinds of people because of its excellent quality. As an example of this, each guitar is carefully made by hand and not produced by machine. It is created with love and care; accordingly, it is made of the finest quality materials. Because of its fine sound, this instrument has been heard around the world. The tone quality is always being improved by musical experts. In addition to structure and sound, this guitar is beautiful to look at because it was hand-painted. Moreover, the wood was polished and the metal was shined.

This style of guitar has been exported to a lot of different countries as a result of its superior quality. It will continue to be bought by many people. In fact, a better guitar cannot be found.

MORE THAN THREE PARAGRAPHS

Focus:
Three- to Five-Paragraph Outline

You have already practiced one- and three-paragraph outlines and compositions. The outlines that show the expansion from one to three paragraphs are presented here again. A five-paragraph outline is just an expansion of a three-paragraph outline. Discuss with your teacher how the examples on page 148 show the relationship between a three-paragraph and five-paragraph outline. Notice how the three-paragraph specifics, i.e., A, B, C, are developed into topic sentences with their own specifics in the five-paragraph format. Also, the transition sentence disappears in the five-paragraph format. Your teacher will point out the suggested sentence distribution for the actual composition as shown below.

One-Paragraph Outline*

Title:	Studying in Another Country
Introduction:	I. There are many good reasons for people to study in a foreign country.
Body:	A. Language B. Culture C. People
Conclusion:	People can broaden their experience and increase their knowledge by studying outside of their countries.

*This one-paragraph *composition* format suggests eight sentences distributed as the following chart indicates:

Introduction:	I. 1 sentence
Body:	A. 2 sentences B. 2 sentences C. 2 sentences
Conclusion:	1 sentence
	8 Total Sentences

Three-Paragraph Outline**

Title:	Studying in Another Country
Introduction:	I. There are many good reasons for people to study in a foreign country.
Transition:	↑ II. ↓ In another country, foreign students can learn about much more than just their major subject.
Body:	A. Language B. Culture C. People
Conclusion:	People can broaden their experience and increase their knowledge by studying outside of their countries.

**This three-paragraph *composition* format suggests thirteen sentences distributed as the following chart indicates:

Introduction:	I.	3 sentences
Transition:	II.	1 sentence
Body:	A.	2 sentences
	B.	2 sentences
	C.	2 sentences
Conclusion:	III.	3 sentences
		13 Total Sentences

Three-Paragraph Outline

Title: Studying in Another Country

Introduction: I. There are many good reasons for people to study in a foreign country.

Transition: II. In another country, foreign students can learn much more than just their major subject.

Body:
- A. Language
- B. Culture
- C. People

Conclusion: III. People can broaden their experience and increase their knowledge by studying abroad.

Three-Paragraph Outline

Introduction:	I.	3 sentences
Transition:	II.	1 sentence
	A.	2 sentences
Body:	B.	2 sentences
	C.	2 sentences
Conclusion:	III.	3 sentences
		13 Total Sentences

This three-paragraph *composition* format suggests thirteen sentences distributed as the following chart indicates:

Five-Paragraph Outline

Title: Studying in Another Country

Introduction: I. There are many good reasons for people to study in a foreign country.

Body:

II. The first reason to have this experience is to learn a new language.
- A. Studies
- B. Practice

III. Another reason is to appreciate a different culture.
- A. Similarities
- B. Differences

IV. A final reason to study in another place is to know and understand people.
- A. Friends
- B. Teachers

Conclusion: V. People can broaden their experience and increase their knowledge by studying abroad.

Five-Paragraph Outline

Introduction:	I.	3 sentences
	II.	1 sentence
	A.	2 sentences
	B.	2 sentences
	III.	1 sentence
Body:	A.	2 sentences
	B.	2 sentences
	IV.	1 sentence
	A.	2 sentences
	B.	2 sentences
Conclusion:	V.	3 sentences
		21 Total Sentences

This five-paragraph *composition* format suggests twenty-one sentences distributed as the following chart indicates:

Focus: *Expanding Three Paragraphs to Five Paragraphs*

You have seen how a three-paragraph outline can develop into a five-paragraph outline. Your teacher can show you that the main difference is the development of the body. In a three-paragraph composition, the body is just *one* paragraph. However, in a five-paragraph composition, the body is expanded into *three* paragraphs. The introduction and conclusion do not have to change. Look at the following outline for a five-paragraph composition. With your teacher and your classmates, fill in the missing sentences that will complete the body of this five-paragraph composition.

Exercise:

Title: Studying in Another Country

Introduction: I. There are many good reasons for people to study in a foreign country.

Body:

II. The first reason to have this experience is to learn a new language.
- A. Studies
- B. Practice

III. Another reason to go to a foreign country is to appreciate a different culture.
- A. Similarities
- B. Differences

IV. A final reason to study in another place is to know and understand other people.
- A. Friends
- B. Teachers

Conclusion: V. People can broaden their experience and increase their knowledge by studying abroad.

Studying in Another Country

I. (1) There are many good reasons for people to study in a foreign country. (2) Students will be exposed to new situations. (3) Lots of knowledge can be gained from this type of experience.

II. (4) The first reason to have this experience is to learn a new language.

(5) ______________________________

(6) ______________________________.

(7) ______________________________.

(8) ______________________________.

III. (9) Another reason to go to a foreign country is to appreciate a different culture. (10) ______________________________

______________________________. (11) ______________

______________________________. (12) ______________

______________________________. (13) ______________

____

IV. (14) A final reason to study in another place is to know and understand other people. (15) ______________________________

____________________. (16) ____________________

____.

(17)____________________________________.

(18)____________________________________.

V. (19) People can broaden their experience and increase their knowledge by studying abroad. (20) Books will not be their only source of knowledge. (21) They will learn many things simply by experiencing the language, the culture, and the people.

Focus:
Five-Paragraph Outline Practice

Fill in the information for these five-paragraph outlines. Then try to write five-paragraph compositions based on your outlines on a separate sheet of paper.

Exercise:

Title: Three Important People in My Life
Introduction: I. ____________________
Body:
II. ____________________
A. ____________________
B. ____________________
III. ____________________
A. ____________________
B. ____________________
IV. ____________________
A. ____________________
B. ____________________
Conclusion: V. ____________________

Title: Three Places to Visit in My Country
Introduction: I. ____________________
Body:
II. ____________________
A. ____________________
B. ____________________
III. ____________________
A. ____________________
B. ____________________
IV. ____________________
A. ____________________
B. ____________________
Conclusion: V. ____________________

COMPOSING FIVE PARAGRAPH COMPOSITIONS

Rhetorical Focus: ***Definition, Exemplification***

Grammar Focus ***Adjectives****

Exercise:

As a practice exercise, look back at some one-paragraph compositions you have already written. Choose several that you enjoy and try to expand them. First, try to develop *introductions* and *conclusions* by changing them from one to three sentences. After that, you can expand the *bodies* by changing them to three paragraphs. Try to do the following example and then go back and choose your own from Chapter 3.

Example:

One paragraph:

Title: My Best Friend

Introduction: I. A person has to be special to be a best friend and "special" means different things to different people.

Body:
- A. Sensitive
- B. Understanding
- C. Reliable

Conclusion: I am lucky to have a friend with these qualities

My Best Friend

A person has to be special to be a best friend and "special" means different things to different people. My companion is special to me because he is sensitive. For instance, he senses when I am unhappy, and he tries to make me feel cheerful. For this reason, I know he is understanding. In other words, I don't have to explain everything to him in detail because he just knows. Furthermore, my best friend is special because of his reliability. As an illustration, he always tries to help people when he can, and all of his friends know they can depend on him. I am lucky to have a friend with these qualities.

Three paragraphs:

Title: My Best Friend

Introduction: I. A person has to be special to be a best friend and "special" means different things to different people.

Transition: II. *For me, a best friend has very specific qualities.*

Body:
- A. Sensitive
- B. Understanding
- C. Considerate

Conclusion: III. I am lucky to have a friend with these qualities.

Exercise:

My Best Friend

A person has to be special to be a best friend and "special" means different things to different people. ______________________________

______________________________. ______________________________

______________________________.

*See pages 103 and 105 for Grammar Review and Context: Adjectives. Also see Appendix H.

For me, a best friend has very specific qualities. My companion is special to me because he is sensitive. He senses when I am unhappy and tries to make me cheerful. For this reason, I know he is understanding. In other words, I don't have to explain everything to him in detail because he just knows. Furthermore, my best friend is special because of his reliability. As an illustration, he always tries to help people when he can, and all of his friends know they can depend on him.

I am lucky to have a friend with these qualities. ______________________
____.
____.

Five paragraphs:

Title: My Best Friend

Introduction: I. A person has to be special to be a best friend and "special" means different things to different people.

Body:

II. For me, a best friend has specific qualities, such as sensitivity.
- A. Attentive
- B. Perceptive

III. Another important trait that makes my friend special is understanding.
- A. Intelligent
- B. Accepting

IV. The last special characteristic that my best friend has is reliability.
- A. Helpful
- B. Consistent

Conclusion: V. I am lucky to have a friend with these qualities.

Exercise:

My Best Friend

A person has to be special to be a best friend and "special" means different things to different people. ______________________________
____________________. ____.

For me, a best friend has specific qualities, such as sensitivity. __________
____. ______________
____.
____
________________. ____
____________________________.

Another important trait that makes my friend special is understanding.
____.

____

_______________. ____

____. _______________

____.

The last special characteristic that my best friend has is reliability.

____

_______________. ____

____. _______________

____.

____

_____________________________________.

I am lucky to have a friend with these qualities. _______________

____. _______________

____.

Rhetorical Focus: ***Description***

Grammar Focus: ***Past Tense****

Exercise:

Write a *five*-paragraph composition based on this three-paragraph description. It might be helpful to write a five-paragraph outline first. Then, write about an important person from your country. Only twenty-one sentences are necessary for this five-paragraph composition. Please use a separate sheet of paper.

Example:

Title: An American Who Has Done Something for Humanity

Introduction: I. Martin Luther King was a black man who dedicated his life to improving the situation of the black people in American society.

Transition: II. In 1955, King first became involved in the civil rights movement.

A. Bus desegregation

Body: B. Organized Southern Christian Leadership Conference

C. Voting Rights Act of 1966

Conclusion: III. In conclusion, Martin Luther King was widely known as a public speaker who discussed many different aspects of civil rights.

An American Who Has Done Something for Humanity

Martin Luther King was a black man who dedicated his life to improving the situation of the black people in American society. He began his career as a Southern Baptist minister in Alabama. Because he had a background in religion, he always directed his actions toward peaceful change.

In 1955, King first became involved in the civil rights movement. He began to support bus desegregation in Montgomery, Alabama, when a black

*See pages 90 and 93 for Grammar Review and Context: Past. Also see Appendix K.

woman refused to give up her seat to a white woman. He led a boycott of the city buses which lasted more than a year; as a result of this, segregated seating on Alabama buses was made unconstitutional. King was also a leader of the Southern Christian Leadership Conference (SCLC), which combined different protest groups in the South. The SCLC was a non-violent protest group, and it was responsible for making discrimination problems public in the South. Similarly, another successful thing that King did was to help get the Voting Rights Act of 1966 passed. This federal act guaranteed the rights of black voters.

In conclusion, Martin Luther King was famous as a public speaker who discussed many different aspects of civil rights. While he was speaking for sanitation workers in Memphis, Tennessee, he was assassinated. Not only the black people, but also the entire world, will continue to remember the good work he did for humanity.

Rhetorical Focus: ***Cause and Effect***

Grammar Focus: ***Future Real Conditionals****

Exercise:

Write a five-paragraph *cause and effect* composition about something that will happen as a direct result of another condition. Make sure to vary your sentence beginnings. Try to limit yourself to twenty-one sentences and to separate causes and effects in your mind. Your teacher will go over difficult vocabulary with you. Please use a separate sheet of paper.

Example:

Title: Consequences of Pollution

Introduction: I. If pollution is not controlled, there will be a lot of negative consequences.

Body:

II. The air will become worse if pollution continues.
   A. Cars
   B. Factories

III. The water is going to get dirtier if the situation persists.
   A. Tankers
   B. Wastes

IV. People's and animals' lives will be endangered with more pollution.
   A. Health
   B. Shelter

Conclusion: V. The world will be a safer place to live if pollution is eliminated.

Consequences of Pollution

If pollution is not controlled, there will be a lot of negative consequences. The environment and all living creatures will suffer. Likewise, the world is going to become an impossible place to survive in.

*See page 135 for Grammar Review and Context: Real Conditionals.

The air will become worse if pollution continues. More cars are being produced, and their exhaust fumes pollute the atmosphere. Skies seem gray and black because of the smog in the air. In addition, factories continue to pump smoke into the air people breathe. If chimneys aren't filtered, the air will get more polluted.

Not only the air, but also the water will get dirtier if this situation persists. Tankers are transporting oil in precious waters. Each time there are oil spills, sea life dies. Moreover, large industrial complexes dispose of their wastes in the ocean. If this goes on, the sea will eventually be full of toxic wastes.

Along with air and water, people's and animals' lives will be endangered by more pollution. Lung diseases will increase if there are unhealthy environmental conditions. People will have respiratory ailments. Furthermore, the balance of nature will be disturbed and animals' natural habitats will be destroyed. In other words, certain species of animals could become extinct.

In conclusion, the world will be a safer place if pollution is eliminated. The environment will be healthier. People and animals will be able to live more harmoniously with their environment.

Appendices

This section provides you with extra practice in problem areas as well as with helpful lists. Your teacher will help you decide which areas are difficult for you and assign you topics from the appendices. Some of the typical problems include *cursive practice* and *parts of speech practice.* You can also improve your written vocabulary and grammar by studying the lists of *adjectives, past tense and past participles of irregular verbs, verbs which don't take -ing, modals, comparisons and superlatives,* and *time words* which signal particular verb tenses.

Appendix A

CURSIVE PRACTICE: CAPITAL LETTERS

Exercise:

Place a piece of paper over this exercise and *trace* how the letters are made by following the *numbers* and the *arrows.*

Appendix B

CURSIVE PRACTICE: SMALL LETTERS

Exercise:

Place a piece of paper over this exercise and *trace* how the letters are made by following the *numbers* and the *arrows*.

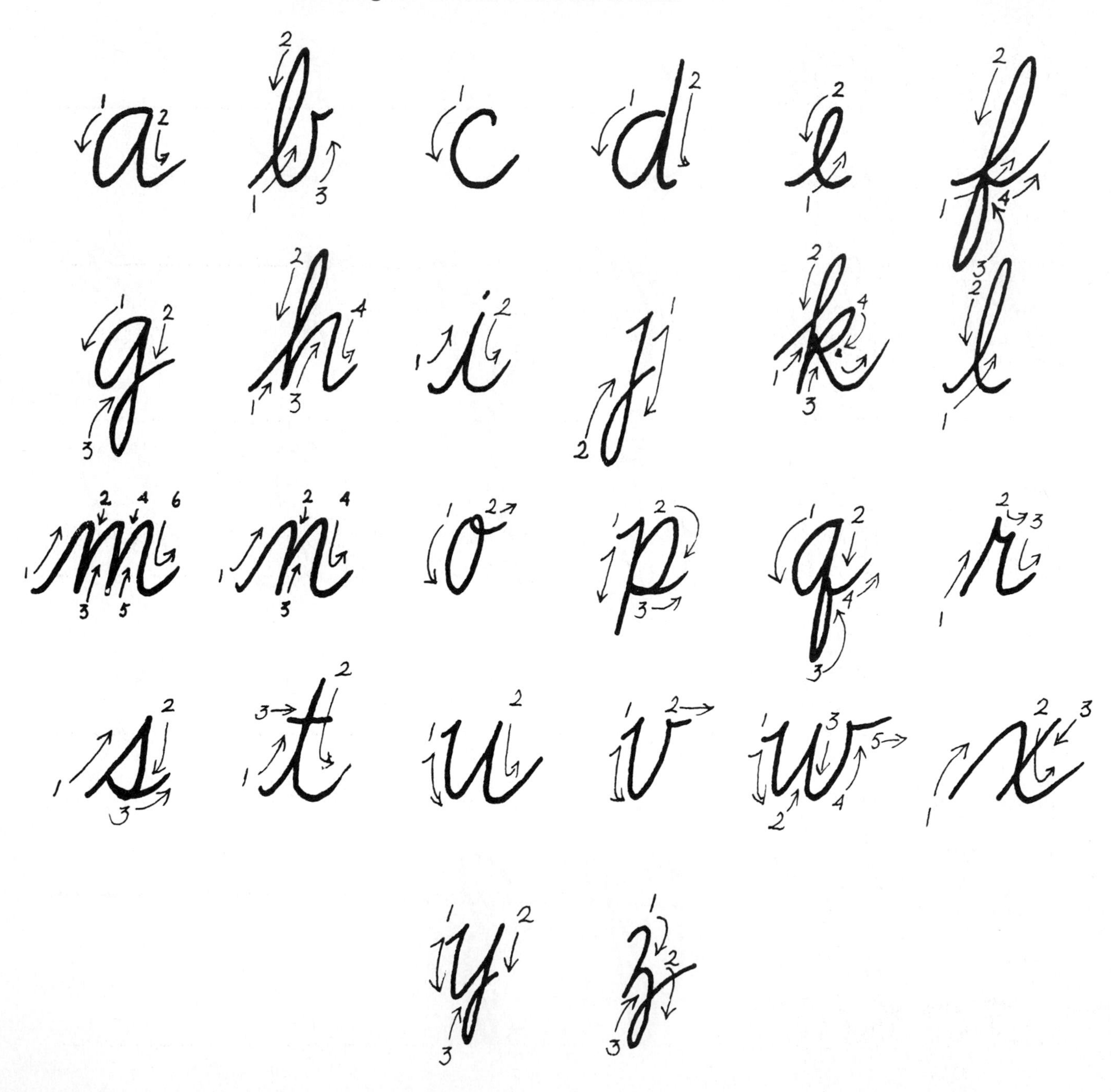

Appendix C

CURSIVE PRACTICE: CAPITAL AND SMALL LETTERS

Exercise:

Practice writing these letters on the line next to the original.

Aa Aa ____________________

Bb Bb ____________________

Cc Cc ____________________

Dd Dd ____________________

Ee Ee ____________________

Ff Ff ____________________

Gg Gg ____________________

Hh *Hh*

Ii *Ii*

Jj *Jj*

Kk *Kk*

Ll *Ll*

Mm *Mm*

Nn *Nn*

Oo *Oo*

Pp *Pp*

Qq *Qq*

Rr *Rr*

Ss *Ss*

Tt *Tt*

Uu *Uu*

V v *V v* ________________

W w *W w* ________________

X x *X x* ________________

Y y *Y y* ________________

Z z *Z z* ________________

Appendix D

CURSIVE PRACTICE: SMALL LETTERS

Exercise:

Practice writing these letters on the line next to the original.

a ______________________

b ______________________

c ______________________

d ______________________

e ______________________

f ______________________

g ______________________

h ______________________

i ______________________

j ______________________

k ______________________

l ______________________

m ______________________

n ______________________

o ________________

p ________________

q ________________

r ________________

s ________________

t ________________

u ________________

v ____________________

w ____________________

x ____________________

y ____________________

z ____________________

Appendix E

CURSIVE PRACTICE IN CONTEXT

Exercise:

Copy the question on one line and *write the answer* on the following line.

What's your name?

Where are you from?

How old are you?

Where do you live?

How many people are in your family?

When did you come to the U.S.A?

What will you study?

Appendix F

PARTS OF SPEECH PRACTICE

Please *identify the parts of speech* in the paragraph given below. The following key and examples will help.

Key:	***Examples:***
Pronoun—**Pro.**	**Pro** *They* are happy.
Adjective—**Adj.**	**Adj.** They are *happy*.
Article—**Art.**	**Art.** *The* boys are happy.
Verb—**V.**	**V.** The boys *are* happy.
Noun—**N.**	**N.** The *boys* are happy.
Adverb—**Adv.**	**Adv.** The boys run *fast*.
Preposition—**Prep.**	**Prep.** The boys run fast *in* the park.
Conjunction—**Conj.**	**Conj.** The boys run *and* walk.

Exercise:

Natalie is a very busy person. She always does many things. For instance, in the morning, she comes to school quickly by car. Then, she teaches from nine to three. In the afternoon, she goes home and rests.

Yesterday, Natalie went to her ceramics class. She made two wine glasses. She is enjoying her class a lot, and she wants to make many things.

Natalie is usually tired because she works and studies. She is a happy person but she is sometimes sleepy.

Appendix G

VERBS THAT DON'T USUALLY OCCUR IN THE PRESENT CONTINUOUS* -ING *FORM

Verbs Showing Emotion and Volition	***Verbs of Possession***
doubt	belong
like	have
love	own
need	
prefer	
want	
Verbs of Perception	***Verbs Showing Characteristics of the Subject***
believe	contain
hear	cost
know	equal
see	fit
seem	include
taste	mean
think	require
understand	

Appendix H

MORE ADJECTIVES IN CONTEXT

1. accidental — He didn't break the glass on purpose. It was *accidental.*
2. active — The baby moves around a lot. She is *active.*
3. angry — When someone insults me, I get *angry.*
4. anxious — When their children stay out late, most parents get *anxious.*
5. attractive — Her clothes always look good. They are *attractive.*
6. automatic — He doesn't have to think because his actions are *automatic.*
7. awkward — He is not graceful. He is *awkward.*
8. bad — The food at that restaurant was *bad.* It was cold and salty.
9. beautiful — The weather in Hawaii is *beautiful.*
10. bitter — Lemons are bitter. Some medicine is *bitter.*
11. brave — The woman who saved her husband from a bear was *brave.*
12. busy — She has to work in an office and do housework. She is *busy.*
13. calm — He doesn't get excited. He is always *calm.*
14. careful — I will only ride with *careful* drivers.
15. careless — I won't ride with *careless* drivers.
16. cheerful — He looks happy all the time. He is even *cheerful* on Monday.
17. casual — He is not formal. He is *casual.*
18. clever — She can fix almost any machine. She is *clever.*
19. complete — Your application is not *complete.* You need to sign it.
20. correct — Your homework is *correct.* There are no mistakes.
21. cool — The Pacific Northwest has a *cool* climate.
22. crazy — That man is *crazy.* He thinks he can fly like a bird.
23. curious — Four-year-old children are *curious* about everything.
24. definite — Her answer is *definite.* She will not change her mind.
25. difficult — Learning to spell English words is *difficult.*
26. doubtful — It is *doubtful* that prices will go down.
27. dry — The climate in Arizona is *dry.*
28. dull — Many T.V. programs are *dull.* They are not interesting.
29. eager — A curious person is *eager* to learn new things.
30. early — They have an *early* class.
31. easy — His accent is *easy* to understand because he speaks clearly.
32. efficient — She is organized and does her work carefully. She's *efficient.*
33. enthusiastic — They are *enthusiastic* about their new house.
34. excellent — The bus service is *excellent.*
35. fast — Mary Decker is a very *fast* runner.
36. famous — Jane Fonda is a *famous* actress.
37. fantastic — The food at that expensive restaurant is *fantastic.*
38. final — The *final* day of class is Friday.
39. frequent — He comes often. He is a *frequent* guest at our house.
40. fresh — *Fresh* orange juice is delicious.
41. foolish — It is *foolish* to carry a lot of money in a purse or wallet.
42. general — The *general* topic is food. The specific subject is fruit.
43. gentle — Mahatma Gandhi was a *gentle* man. He wasn't violent.
44. glad — She said, "I'm *glad* to meet you." She was pleased to meet me.
45. good — We had a *good* time at the party.
46. graceful — The ballet dancer moved beautifully. She was *graceful.* She wasn't awkward.
47. greedy — He wants more than he needs. He is *greedy* and not generous.

48. happy She will be *happy* when she sees her family again.
49. hard The work is easy, but he says it is *hard* because he is lazy.
50. healthy He rests, exercises, and eats nutritious food. He is *healthy*.
51. heavy The bag weighed 80 pounds. It was *heavy*.
52. honest He doesn't tell the truth. He lies. He isn't *honest*.
53. hot The climate of Kuwait is *hot*.
54. hungry I didn't eat breakfast or lunch. I'm *hungry*.
55. impatient She doesn't like to sit or wait a long time. She is *impatient*.
56. impolite Ronnie interrupted Walter three times. Ronnie was *impolite*.
57. industrious They are hard-working. They are *industrious* and not lazy.
58. inexpensive His watch wasn't cheap, but it was *inexpensive*.
59. intelligent Helen is smart. She isn't stupid. She's *intelligent*.
60. interesting Visiting different countries is very *interesting*.
61. illegal It is *illegal* to drive when the light is red.
62. kind She never hurts anyone. She is *kind*.
63. late The teacher doesn't accept *late* homework.
64. legal It is not *legal* for minors to enter taverns because they are too young.
65. logical She has a *logical* mind. She thinks clearly.
66. loud We hate *loud* noises. We prefer soft noises or silence.
67. messy He isn't neat. He is *messy*.
68. miserable They are unhappy. They are *miserable*.
69. neat His outlines and compositions are always *neat*.
70. necessary It's *necessary* to practice English outside of class.
71. nervous Actors are usually *nervous* before they go on stage.
72. new Are you going to buy a *new* car or a used car?
73. noisy He's almost never quiet. He's *noisy*.
74. occasional She sometimes visits us. She's an *occasional* visitor.
75. permanent I need to know your *permanent* address, not your temporary one.
76. polite We prefer *polite* people to rude ones.
77. poor Would you rather be rich and sick or *poor* and healthy?
78. possible Do you think it's *possible* that creatures from Mars will visit?
79. practical She is not a dreamer. She is very *practical*.
80. pretty The picture of the flowers is very *pretty*.
81. probable I'm not sure but the *probable* answer is that she's sick.
82. prompt They are always on time. They are *prompt*.
83. proper Are pajamas the *proper* thing to wear to a party?
84. proud She is a good student, and her parents are *proud* of her.
85. quick She has a *quick* mind.
86. quiet The library should be a *quiet* place.
87. rapid He is a *rapid* reader. He reads faster than I do.
88. rare People who can write with both hands are *rare*.
89. ready Are you *ready* to go?
90. real Do you like to smell *real* flowers or plastic flowers?
91. reckless The *reckless* motorcycle rider finally had an accident.
92. regular My *regular* breakfast includes eggs, potatoes, toast, and coffee.
93. rude It's *rude* to sit on a bus when an older person is standing.
94. sad He is *sad* because he couldn't see his friends before they left.
95. safe It isn't *safe* to walk down dark alleys at night.
96. sharp The knife is *sharp*.
97. silent If you can't think of a nice thing to say, it's better to be *silent*.
98. sincere You can trust him. He's *sincere*.
99. simple We have a *simple* lunch and a big supper.
100. skillful Kareem Abdul-Jabbar is a very *skillful* basketball player.
101. sleepy He didn't sleep very well and now he looks *sleepy*.
102. sloppy His clothes are on the floor. He's *sloppy*.
103. soft A baby's skin is very *soft*.
104. superb Julia Child is a *superb* cook.

105. tasty	The food is delicious. It is very *tasty*.
106. terrible	That was a *terrible* accident! Four people died.
107. terrific	She is a *terrific* athlete. When she plays, her team always wins.
108. tired	You worked hard last night, and you look *tired* today.
109. true	It is not a lie. It is a *true* story.
110. thrifty	They spend their money carefully. They are *thrifty*.
111. thoughtful	She always remembers my birthday. She's a *thoughtful* person.
112. tough	They are *tough* instructors because they give lots of homework and exams.
113. tight	His pants felt *tight* after he ate a big dinner.
114. timid	The new student was *timid* in class and didn't talk much.
115. transparent	The glass is *transparent*. I can see through it.
116. tricky	The police can't catch the thief because he is so *tricky*.
117. ugly	It was raining, cold, and dark outside. I thought it was an *ugly* day.
118. unusual	It is *unusual* not to wear shoes in the winter.
119. unkind	Many people are *unkind* to animals. They treat them badly.
120. unfair	It was an *unfair* test. There were fifteen pages and only one hour to do it.
121. unhappy	She is an *unhappy* person. She never smiles.
122. upset	The children are crying. They must be *upset*.
123. urgent	The student received an *urgent* message to call home.
124. useful	Dictionaries are *useful* when you study a foreign language.
125. valuable	Diamonds are *valuable* gems. They cost a lot of money.
126. vacant	That apartment is *vacant*. We can speak to the manager about it.
127. variable	The weather is changeable. There are *variable* winds.
128. violent	He is a *violent* man. He killed many people.
129. warm	It's not too hot or too cold. In other words, it's *warm*.
130. wasteful	Don't be *wasteful*. Turn off the lights when you leave.
131. weak	Popeye is *weak* when he doesn't eat his spinach.
132. wealthy	He has a Rolls Royce and a big house. He's a *wealthy* man.
133. weird	Some people think modern music is *weird*.
134. wet	I forgot my umbrella so my clothes are *wet*.
135. whole	He ate the *whole* thing! His plate was clean.
136. wild	There are many *wild* animals in the jungle.
137. windy	If it's *windy*, we can go sailing.
138. wise	Older people are *wise* and owls are too.
139. young	They aren't old. On the contrary, they are *young*.
140. zany	That comedian does wild and crazy things. He is *zany*.

Appendix I

MODALS: PRESENT AND FUTURE

Modal	*Equivalent*	*Examples in Context*
can **cannot (can't)**	1. Present ability 2. Informal permission	1. She *can* play guitar, but she *cannot* read music. 2. If you finish your homework, you *can* go.
could ***could not (couldn't)***	1. Past ability 2. Formal request (present, future)	1. I *couldn't* vote when I was a child. 2. *Could* you please help me this week?
should, ought to ***should not (shouldn't), ought not to***	1. Present and future advice 2. Expectation	1. We are tired so we *should* rest. 2. The letter *ought to* arrive today.
had better ***had better not***	1. Strong advice (possible future negative consequence)	1. They *had better not* drive too quickly or they will get a speeding ticket.
must ***must not (mustn't)***	1. Present and future necessity 2. Present probability	1. You *must* study hard for the exam. 2. He has been absent three days. He *must* be sick.
have to ***do, does not have to (don't, doesn't have to)***	1. Present and future necessity 2. Negative—lack of necessity	1. You *have to* study hard for the exam. 2. You *don't have to* go if you don't want to.
may ***may not***	1. Present and future possibility 2. Formal permission	1. The sky is dark. It *may* rain later. 2. *May* I please be excused?
might ***might not***	1. Present and future possibility 2. Very formal permission	1. The sky is dark. It *might* rain later. 2. *Might* I ask you a question?

Appendix J

COMPARISONS AND SUPERLATIVES

COMPARATIVE FORM			SUPERLATIVE FORM		
One Syllable			***One Syllable***		
	Adjectives;	***Adverbs***		***Adjectives;***	***Adverbs***
+	clearer;	more clearly	+	the clearest;	the most clearly
+	finer;	more finely	+	the finest;	the most finely
+	stronger;	more strongly	+	the strongest;	the most strongly
−	less clear;	less clearly	−	the least clear;	the least clearly
−	less fine;	less finely	−	the least fine;	the least finely
−	less strong;	less strongly	−	the least strong;	the least strongly
Two Syllables Ending in -y			***Two Syllables Ending in -y***		
	Adjectives;	***Adverbs***		***Adjectives;***	***Adverbs***
+	happier;	more happily	+	the happiest;	the most happily
+	lazier;	more lazily	+	the laziest;	the most lazily
−	less happy;	less happily	−	the least happy;	the least happily
−	less lazy;	less lazily	−	the least lazy;	the least lazily
Two or More Syllables			***Two or More Syllables***		
	Adjectives;	***Adverbs***		***Adjectives;***	***Adverbs***
+	more careless;	more carelessly	+	the most careless;	the most carelessly
+	more intelligent;	more intelligently	+	the most intelligent;	the most intelligently
+	more enthu-siastic;	more enthu-siastically	+	the most enthu-siastic;	the most enthu-siastically
−	less careless;	less carelessly	−	the least careless;	the least carelessly
−	less intelligent;	less intelligently	−	the least intelligent;	the least intelligently
−	less enthusiastic;	less enthusiastically	−	the least enthusiastic;	the least enthusiastically
Irregular Forms			***Irregular Forms***		
	Adjectives;	***Adverbs***		***Adjectives;***	***Adverbs***
+	better;	better	+	the best;	the best
+	farther;	farther	+	the farthest;	the farthest
+	further;	further	+	the furthest;	the furthest
−	worse;	worse	−	the worst;	the worst

Appendix K

COMMON IRREGULAR VERBS

Simple Form	*Past*	*Past Participle*
arise	arose	arisen
be	was, were	been
beat	beat	beaten
become	became	become
begin	began	begun
bend	bent	bent
bet	bet	bet
bite	bit	bit(ten)
bleed	bled	bled
blow	blew	blown
break	broke	broken
bring	brought	brought
build	built	built
buy	bought	bought
catch	caught	caught
choose	chose	chosen
come	came	come
cost	cost	cost
cut	cut	cut
dig	dug	dug
do	did	done
draw	drew	drawn
drink	drank	drunk
drive	drove	driven
eat	ate	eaten
fall	fell	fallen
feed	fed	fed
feel	felt	felt
fight	fought	fought
find	found	found
fly	flew	flown
forget	forgot	forgot(ten)
forgive	forgave	forgiven
freeze	froze	frozen
get	got	got(ten)
give	gave	given
go	went	gone
grow	grew	grown
hang	hung	hung
have	had	had
hear	heard	heard
hide	hid	hidden

Simple Form	*Past*	*Past Participle*
hit	hit	hit
hold	held	held
hurt	hurt	hurt
keep	kept	kept
know	knew	known
lay	laid	laid
lead	led	led
leave	left	left
let	let	let
lie	lay	lain
light	lighted, lit	lighted, lit
lose	lost	lost
make	made	made
mean	meant	meant
meet	met	met
pay	paid	paid
put	put	put
quit	quit	quit
read	read	read
ride	rode	ridden
ring	rang	rung
run	ran	run
say	said	said
see	saw	seen
sell	sold	sold
send	sent	sent
shake	shook	shaken
shine	shone	shone
shoot	shot	shot
show	showed	showed, shown
shut	shut	shut
sing	sang	sung
sink	sank	sunk
sit	sat	sat
sleep	slept	slept
speak	spoke	spoken
speed	sped	sped
spend	spent	spent
stand	stood	stood
steal	stole	stolen
sweep	swept	swept
swim	swam	swum
swing	swing	swung
take	took	taken
teach	taught	taught
tear	tore	torn
tell	told	told
think	thought	thought
throw	threw	thrown
wake	woke	woke
wear	wore	worn
win	won	won
write	wrote	written

Appendix L

TIME WORDS FOR VERB TENSES

Simple Present	***Simple Past***	***Present Continuous***
every	yesterday	now
usually, sometimes, never, always, seldom, often	last ______	at present
still	______ ago	at the moment
anymore	when	presently
	during	right now
	the ______ before ______	immediately
		today

Past Continuous	***Future***	***Present Perfect***	
while, when	next	already	up to now
during	in	yet	the last ______
yesterday	a ______ from now	recently	today
from ______ to ______	the following ______	lately	for
from ______ until ______	tonight	so far	since
	soon	until now	this ______
			just

Present Perfect Continuous		
all ______ long	for	lately
since	the last ______	recently